Twenty-Two Horses, Stags and Bison

TWENTY-TWO HORSES, STAGS AND BISON

VALENTINA DUBASKY

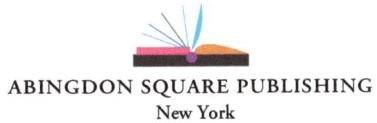

ABINGDON SQUARE PUBLISHING
New York

Artwork © 2017 by Valentina DuBasky

Twenty-Two Horses, Stags and Bison
published by
Abingdon Square Publishing
463 West Street, Suite G122
New York, NY 10014
USA
www.abingdonsquarepublishing.com
Book design: Abingdon Square Publishing

ISBN: 978-0-9830762-8-5
Library of Congress Control Number: 2017945539

Printed in the United States of America

Front Cover: *Winged Horse and Figures,* mixed media on plaster and paper, 30.5 x 33 inches, 2017
Back Cover: *Claret Stag in Russet Field,* oil on paper, 31 x 26 inches, 2012

TABLE OF CONTENTS

ARTIST'S STATEMENT

The inspiration for the horse, stag and bison paintings began one night during a walk in Vermont. Under a full moon, I saw several large, table-sized white cows in a field whose shapes and outlines appeared to be perfect rectangles. As the idea of the animal entered my imagination, I found compelling associations between the horses and bison of the ancient cave paintings and the art of our own time. My horse, stag and bison paintings are balanced between ancient, totemic art and the contemporary imagination. Painted with thick impasto oil paint, and positioned on the edge of abstraction, the paintings can be read as animal, still life, landscape or abstraction.

The new paintings in this series have been inspired by my recent visit to India through the Fulbright Specialist Program. The Indian Himalayas and the Nanda Devi Peak in Uttarakhand provided fresh inspiration for my paintings, and the open-air Shekhawati frescoes in Rajasthan rekindled my interest in artistic exchange and travel along the Silk Route.

I started traveling along the Silk Route to see Buddhist cave paintings and to prepare for my own "modern-day, cave wall paintings" early on in my career as an artist. My first solo trip to the painted Mogao caves near the Dunhuang oasis in western China was followed by a visit to the vivid Ajanta caves in India. I was moved by the beauty of the painted lines and washes of color traversing the strata-like surfaces of the cave walls. The more I observed the cave images, the more complex I found the emotional pull—empty and full at the same time. Additional journeys to the Pech Merle caves in France, the petroglyphs of Sarmishay Gorge in Uzbekistan and the Pang Mapha archaeological site in Northern Thailand near the Myanmar border provided opportunities to see ancient art firsthand and to gather inspiration for new paintings.

Ancient art is a part of nature, created within a specific landscape—mountains, desert, meadow, river and sky. On a purely physical level, the elements of these far-off landscapes provided the raw materials to make the cave art and I could imagine the possibilities for expression in the chorus of mineral pigments that are reflected back from the surrounding hillsides. The light of the Silk Route is unique in each place I visited—the dim light in caves, the clearest light of the mountains, the wide-angle light of deserts remind me that art is inseparable from the mystery and fluidity of perception. Memory, identity, history, and the animals are all written on, and inscribed within, the landscape. The landscapes become "sites" for visual discovery and offer more ideas for the painting.

I start with color—persimmon, claret, amber, sienna, rust, plum and cerulean with marks of turquoise and black. The horses, stags and bison are placed within an abstract, physical landscape, in which paint or plaster suggest strata and provide a context for pictographic notation. Brush marks are painted on, in, and over—or incised into—plaster, or painted within many layers of paint, allowing the strata-like surface to both reveal and conceal the animals and figures. Washes, stains, drips and erasures question what is present and absent. In some of the paintings, rectangles are split or divided and combined with marks, spots and gestures to provide multiple meanings. Incised marks, impasto paint and brush marks suggest the markings of the animal, objects on a table or elements within a landscape. The relationship between myth, totemic art and the unconscious mind, guides the process.

The artwork in this book includes both a monotype and several paintings done in watercolor and ink. Over the years, I have created monotype portfolios and print editions with Pelavin Editions Ltd, Solo Press, and Tandem Press where I have had opportunities to explore animal and Silk Route motifs using print, chine-collé, and encaustic. Together, the paintings, monotype, and drawings complete the body of work.

I cannot help but think that the horses, stags and bison have been with us for a long time. They have accompanied us on our collective, human journey from the caves to the present. In our own time, these creatures still enter our imagination mythically, bringing a sense of wonder, power and delight.

Valentina DuBasky
New York, 2017

PAINTINGS

HORSE WITH FIGURE
Oil on paper, 15.75 x 23 inches, 2017

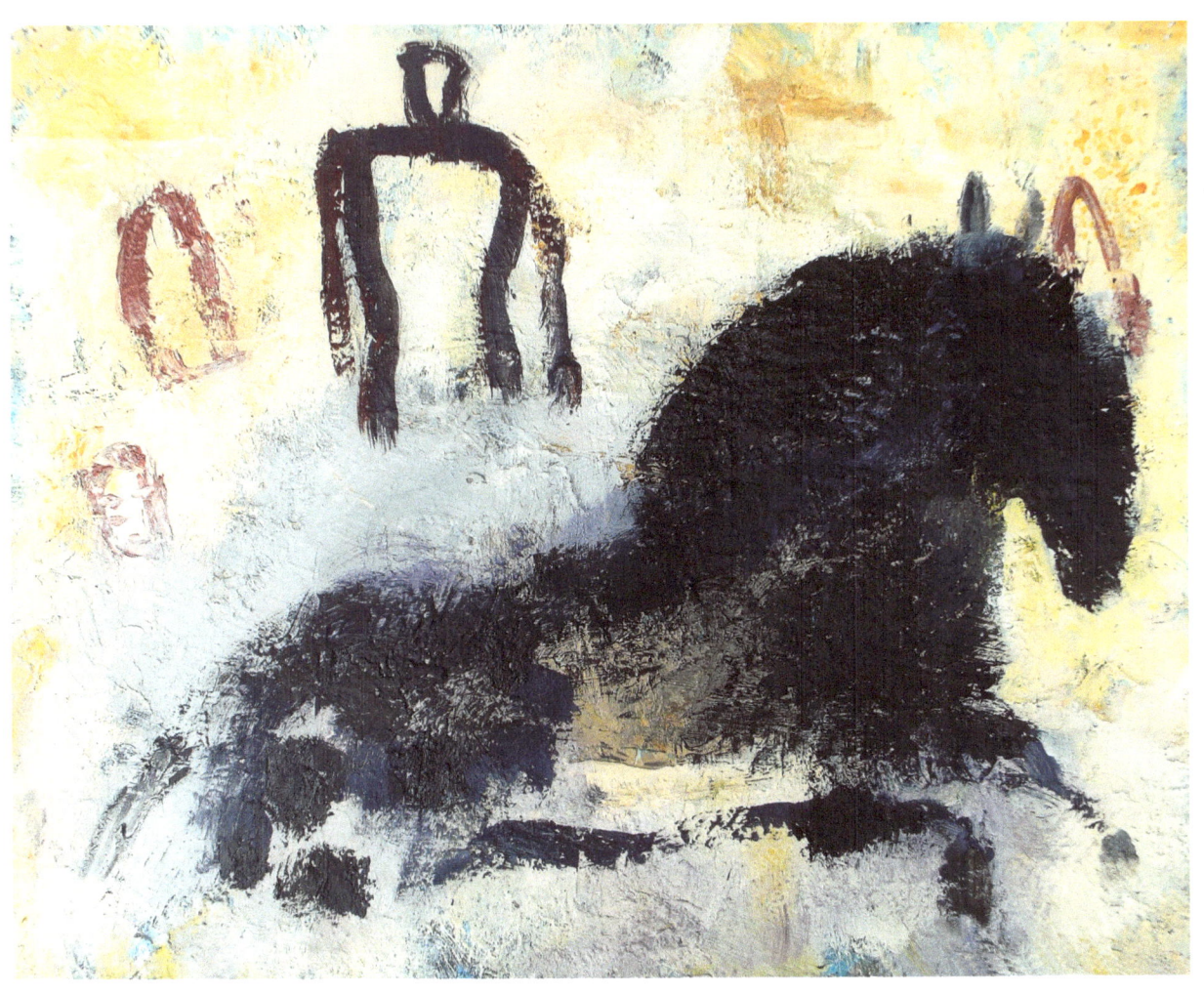

HORSE AND FIGURES IN ROSE FIELD
Oil on paper, 21.75 x 26 inches, 2017

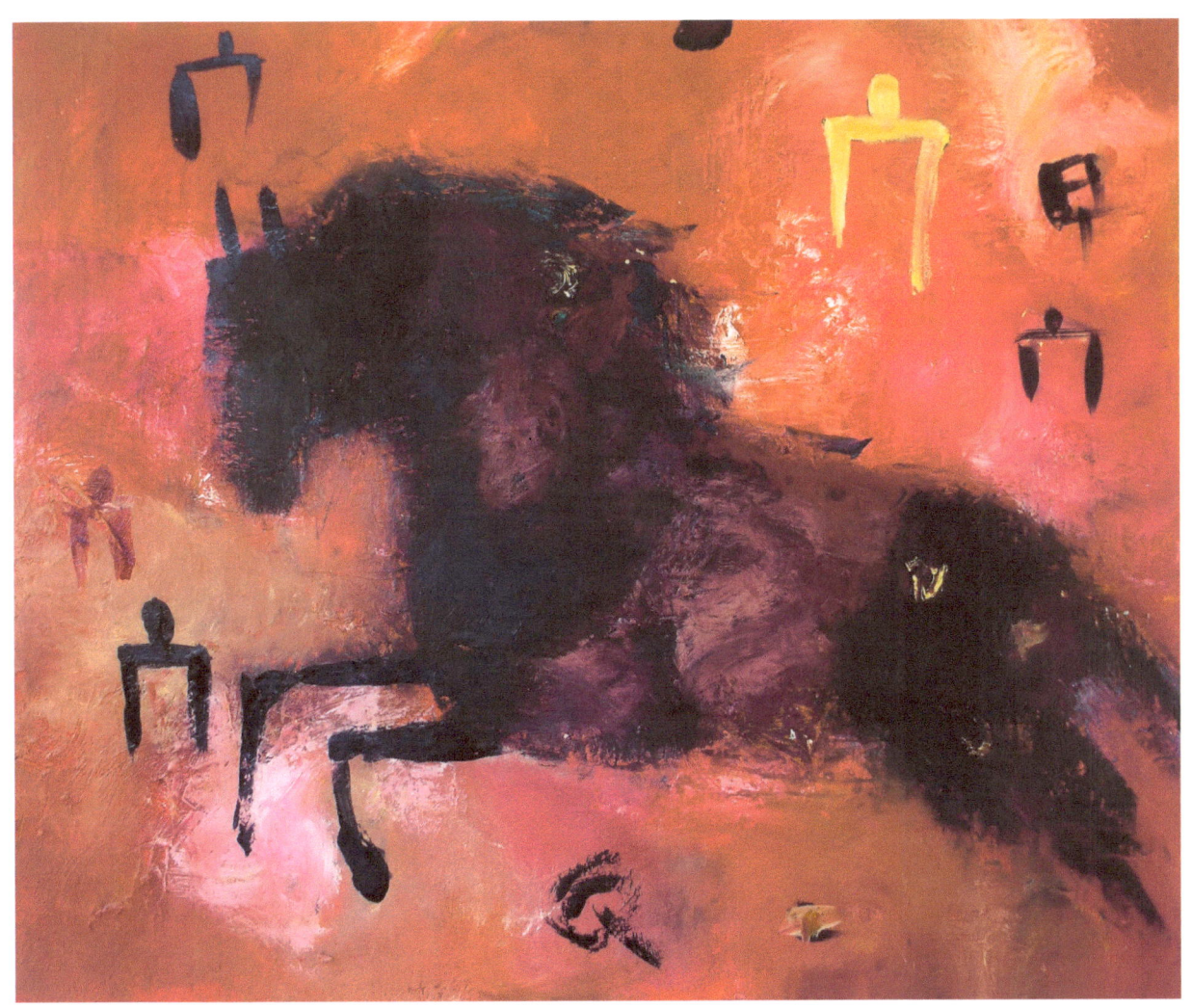

DOUBLE IMAGE IN RED FIELD
Oil on paper, 21.75 x 26 inches, 2017

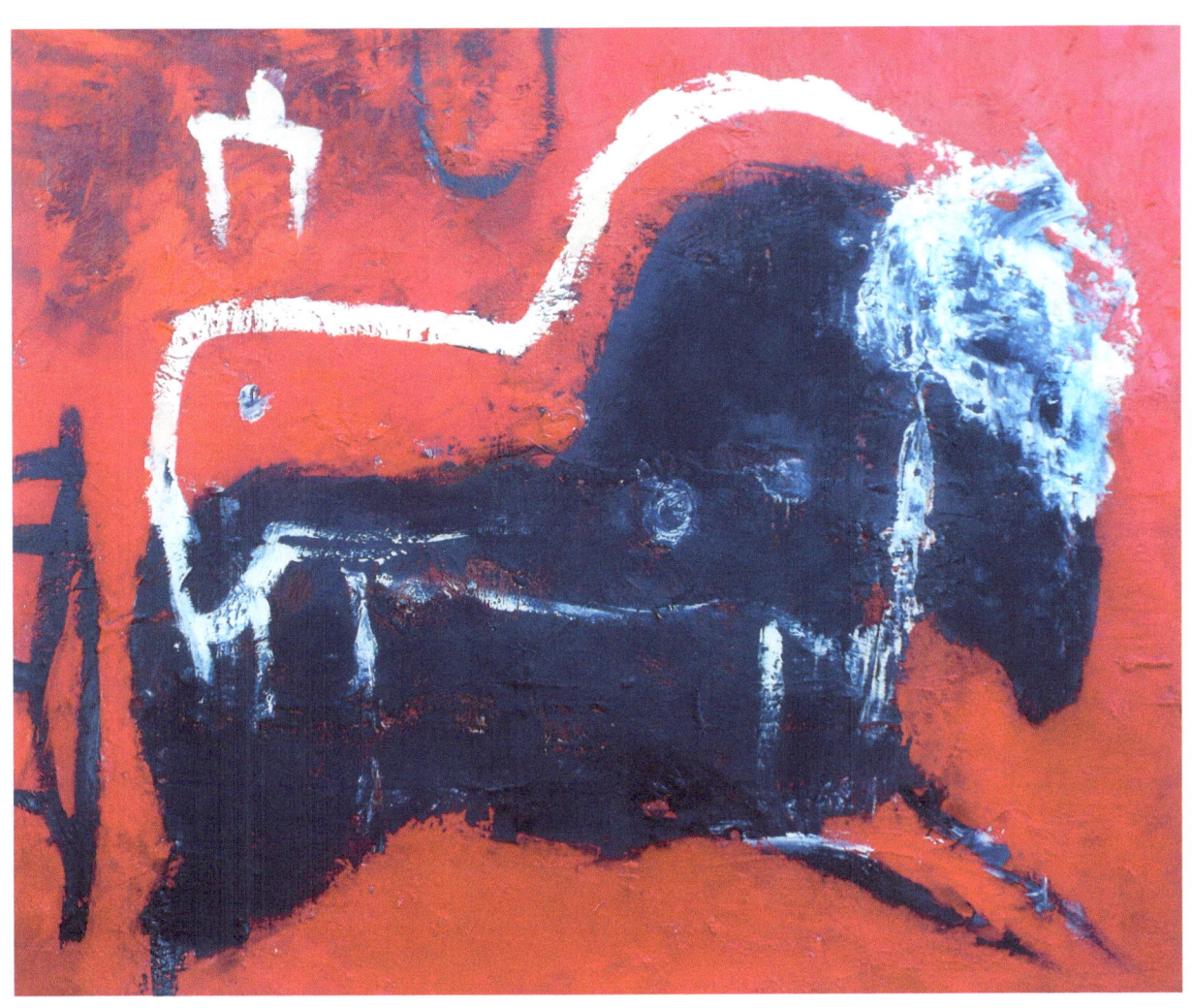

HORSE AND FIGURES IN GREY FIELD
Oil on paper, 21 x 24.75 inches, 2017

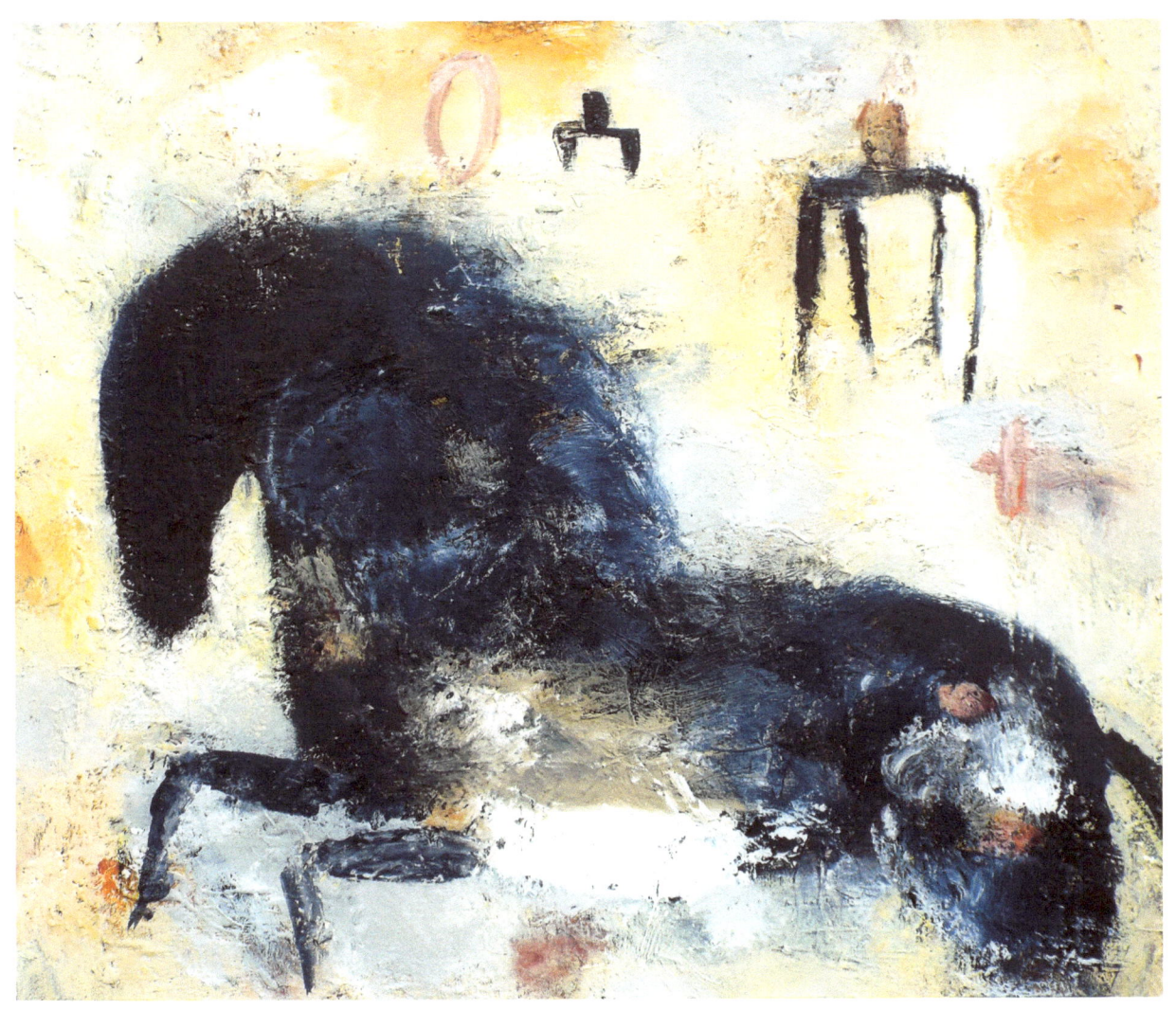

DOUBLE IMAGE IN BLUE FIELD
Oil on paper, 22.5 x 30 inches, 2017

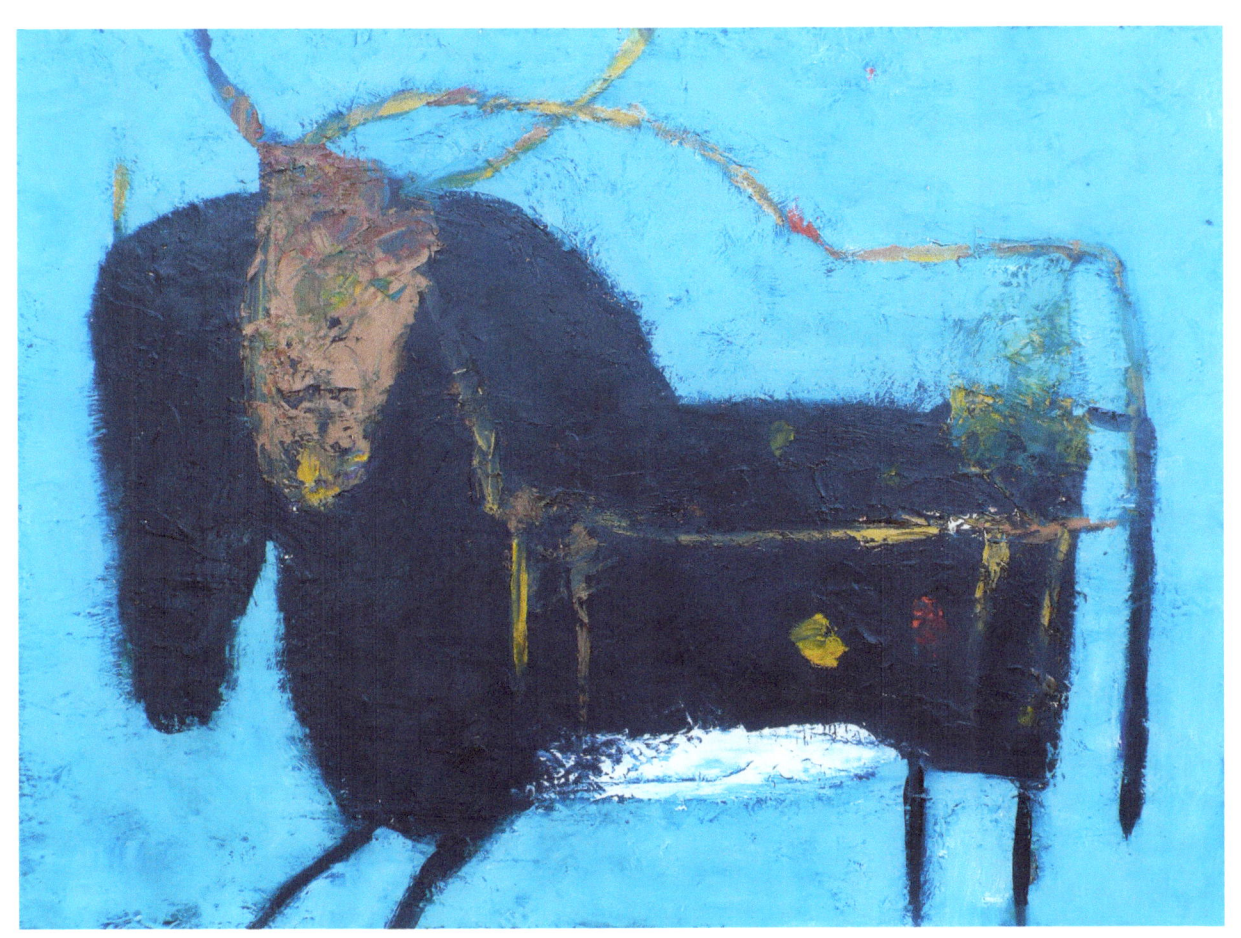

WINGED HORSE AND FIGURES
Mixed media on plaster and paper, 30.5 x 33 inches, 2017

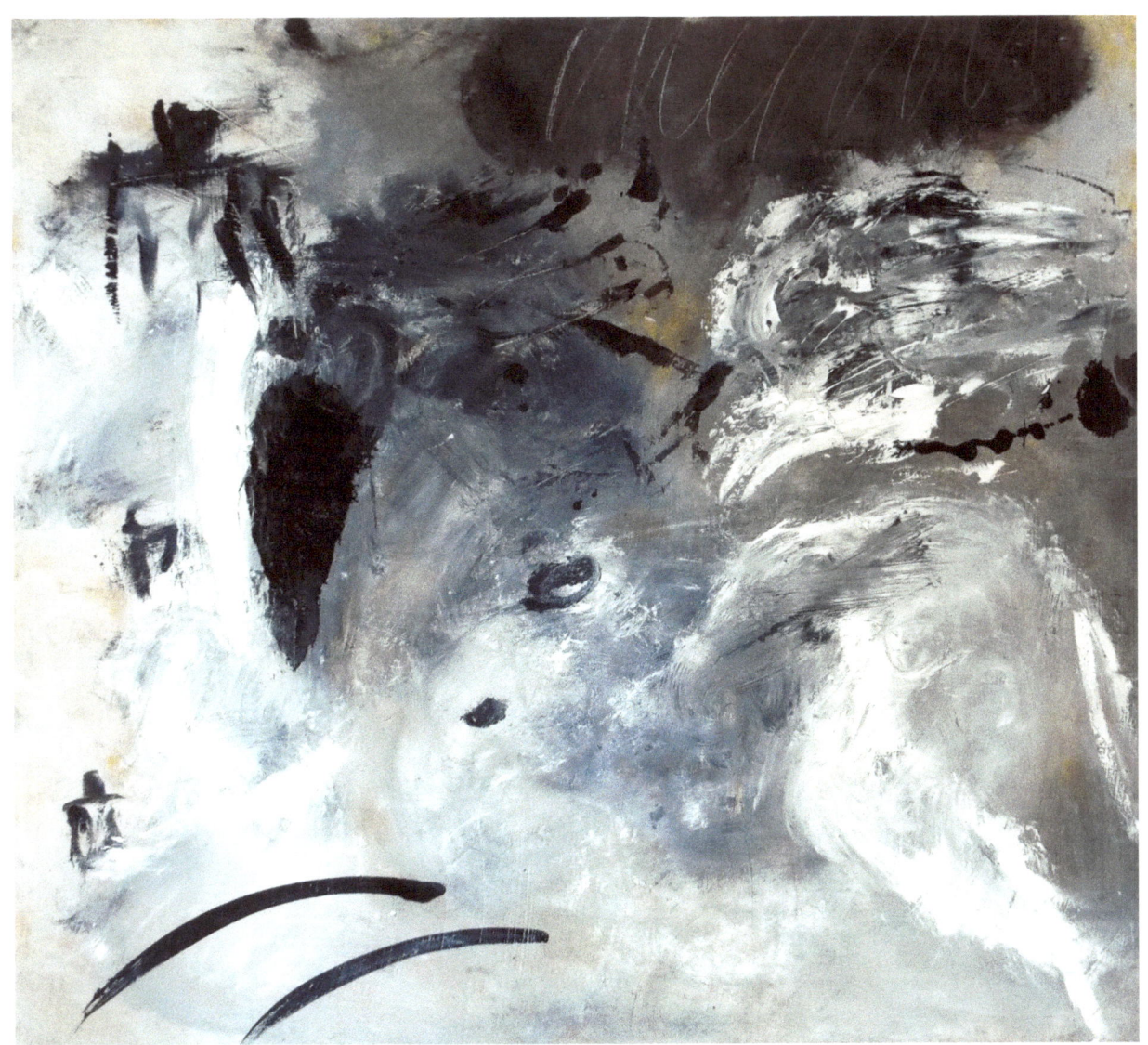

BISON
Mixed media on plaster and paper, 30.5 x 32.5 inches, 2017

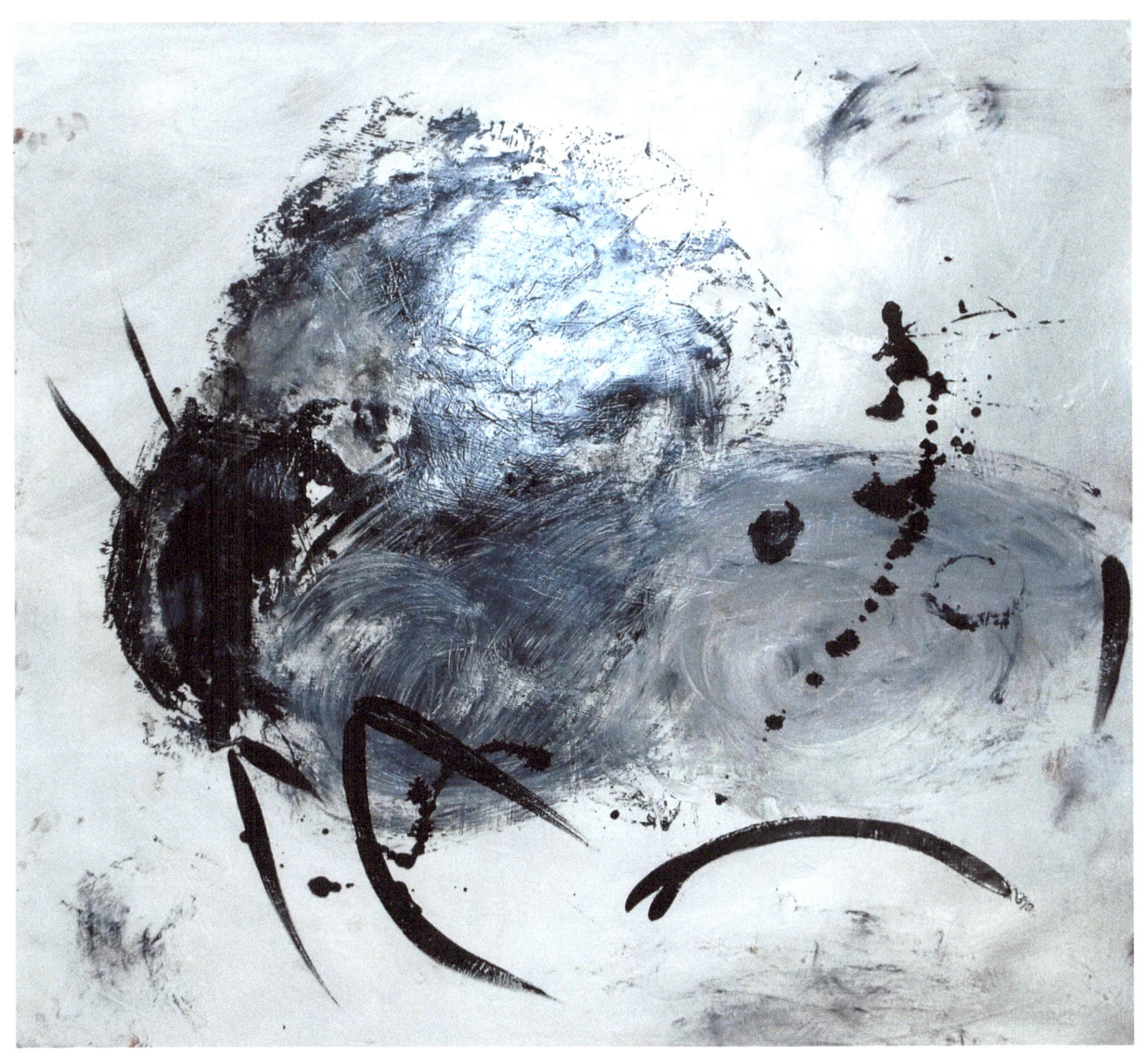

GREY STAG IN RUSSET FIELD
Oil on paper, 31 x 26 inches, 2012

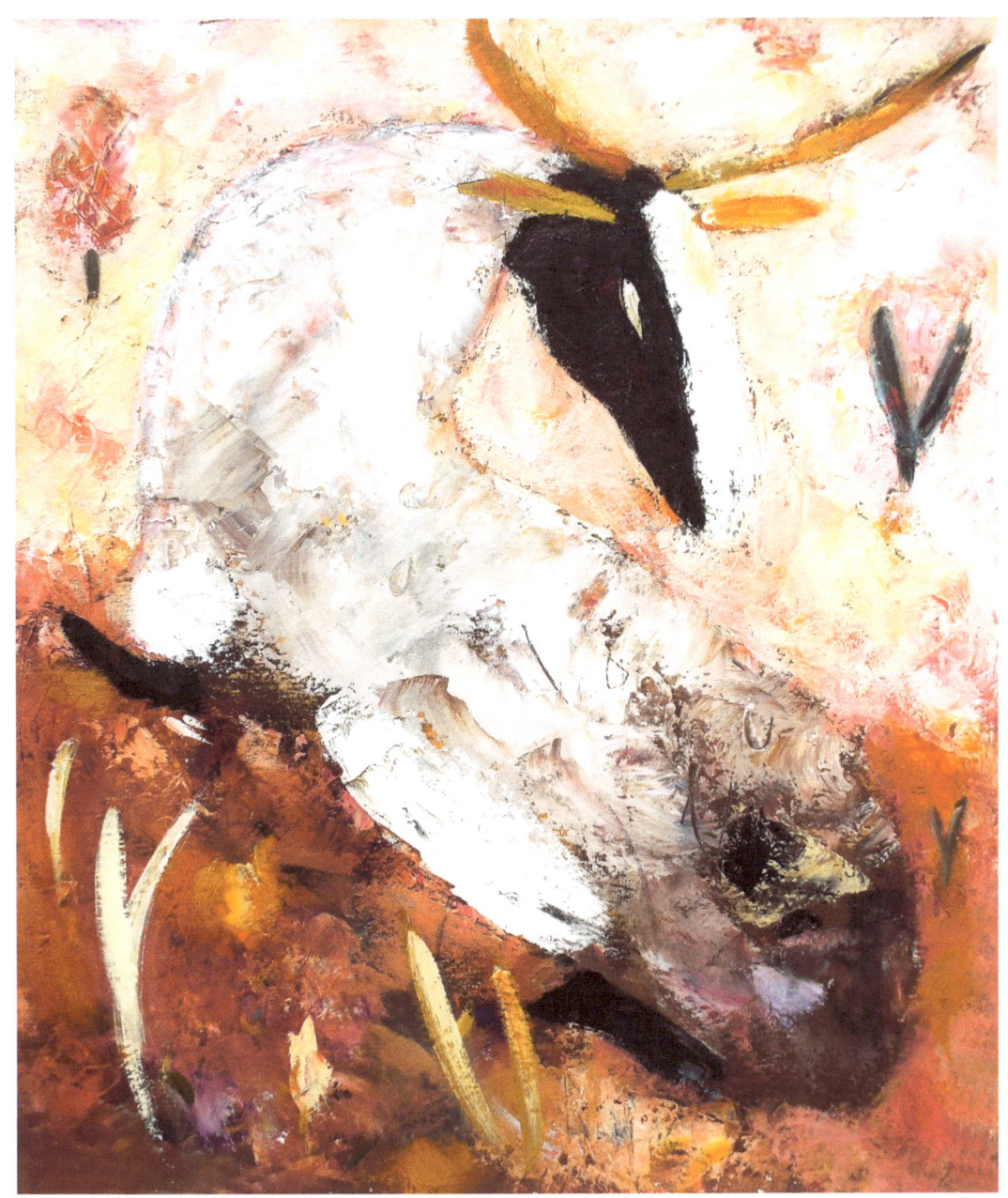

CLARET STAG IN RUSSET FIELD
Oil on paper, 31 x 26 inches, 2012

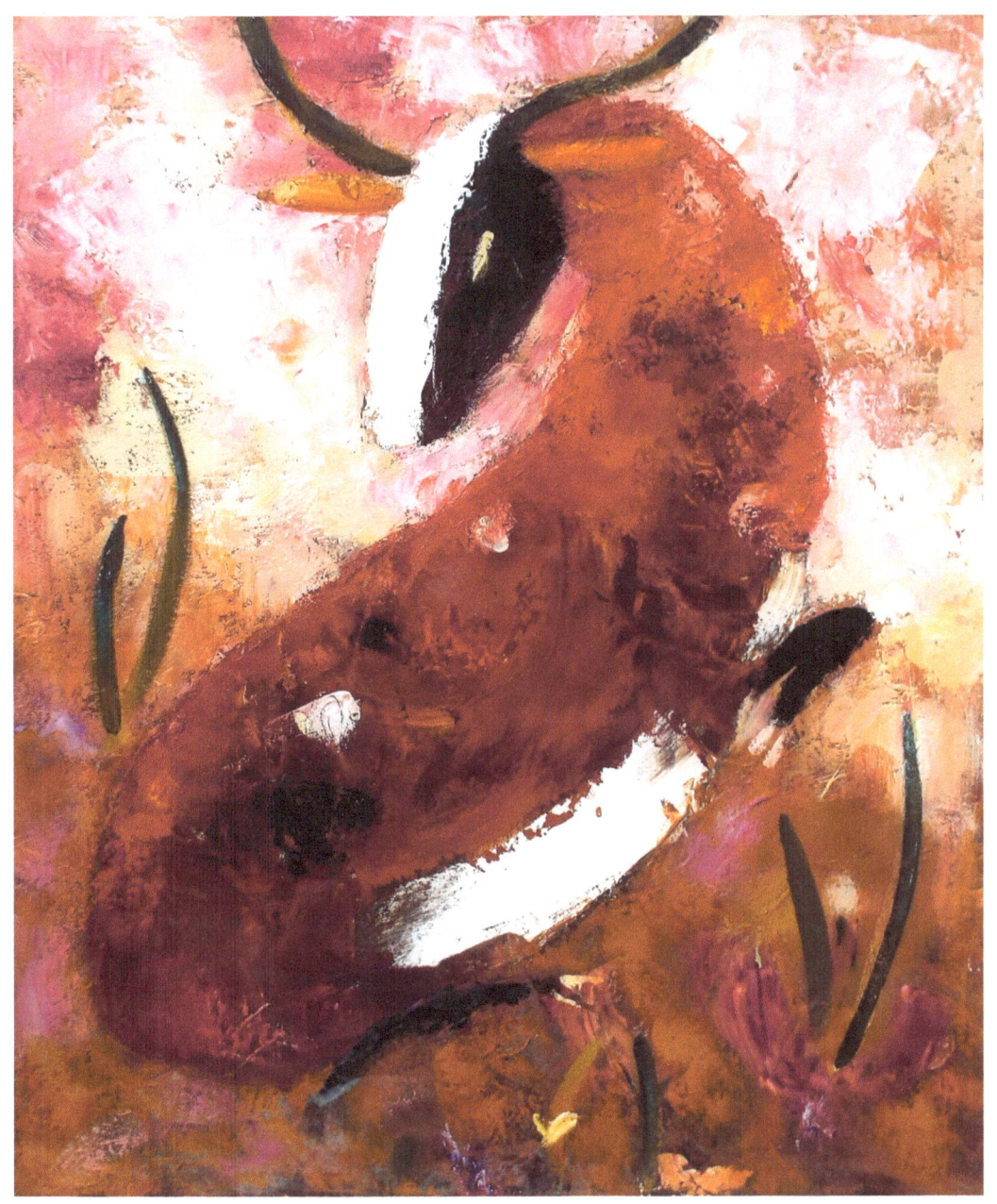

SPOTTED HORSE IN CLARET FIELD
Oil on canvas, 22 x 30 inches, 2016

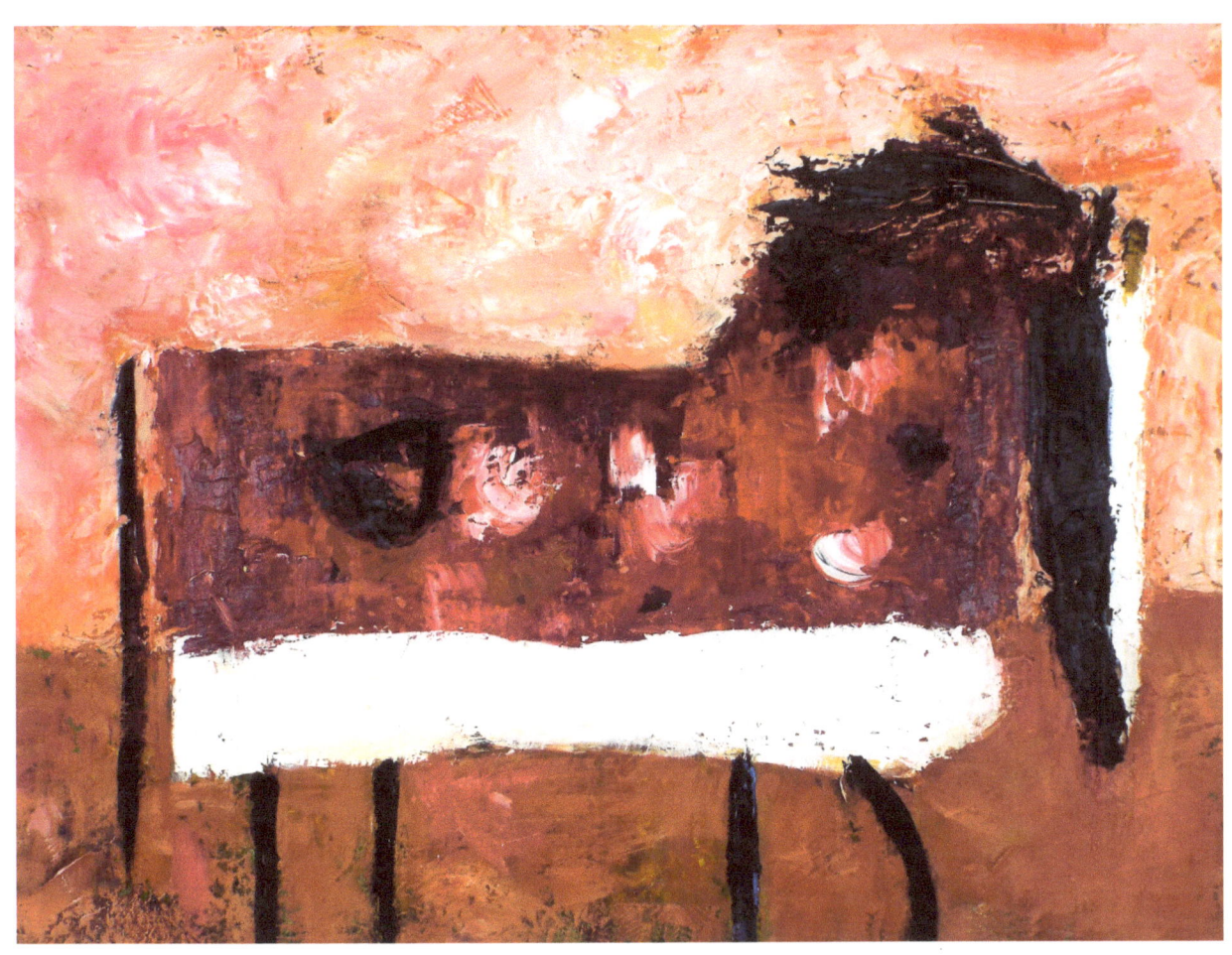

RED SPLIT HORSE
Oil on canvas, 22 x 30 inches, 2016

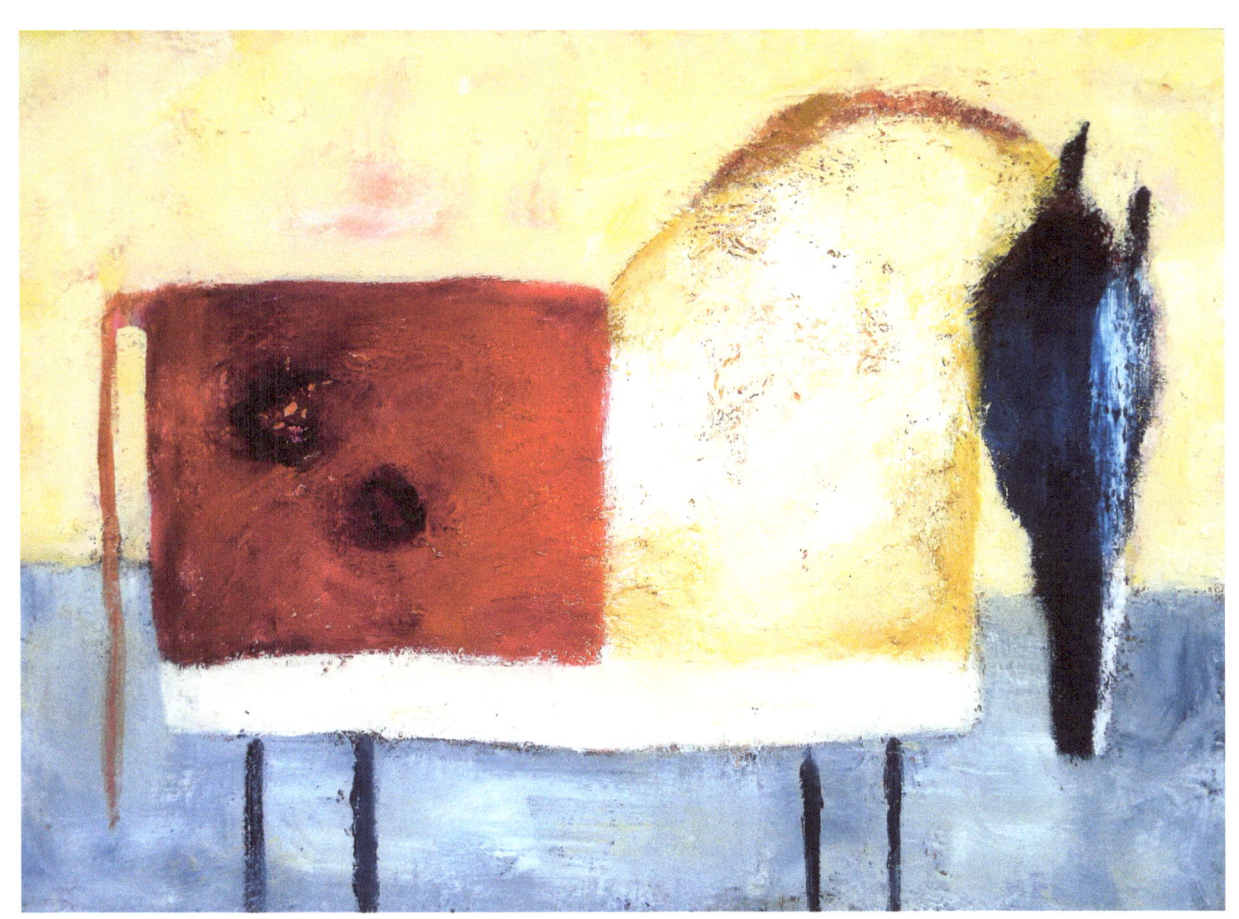

CERULEAN AND WHITE SPOTTED HORSE
Oil on paper, 22.5 x 30 inches, 2017

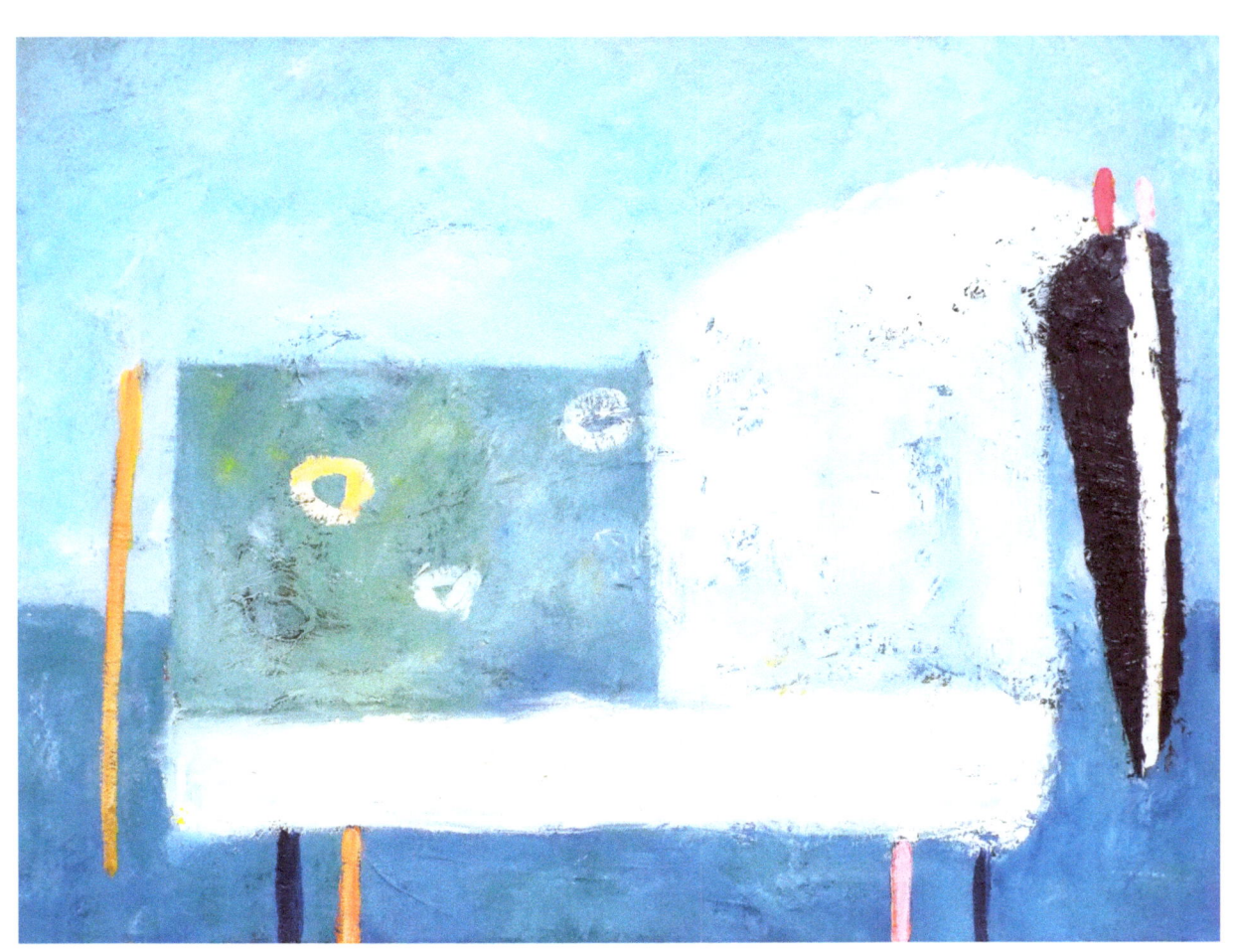

AMBER HORSE
Oil on canvas, 22 x 30 inches, 2016

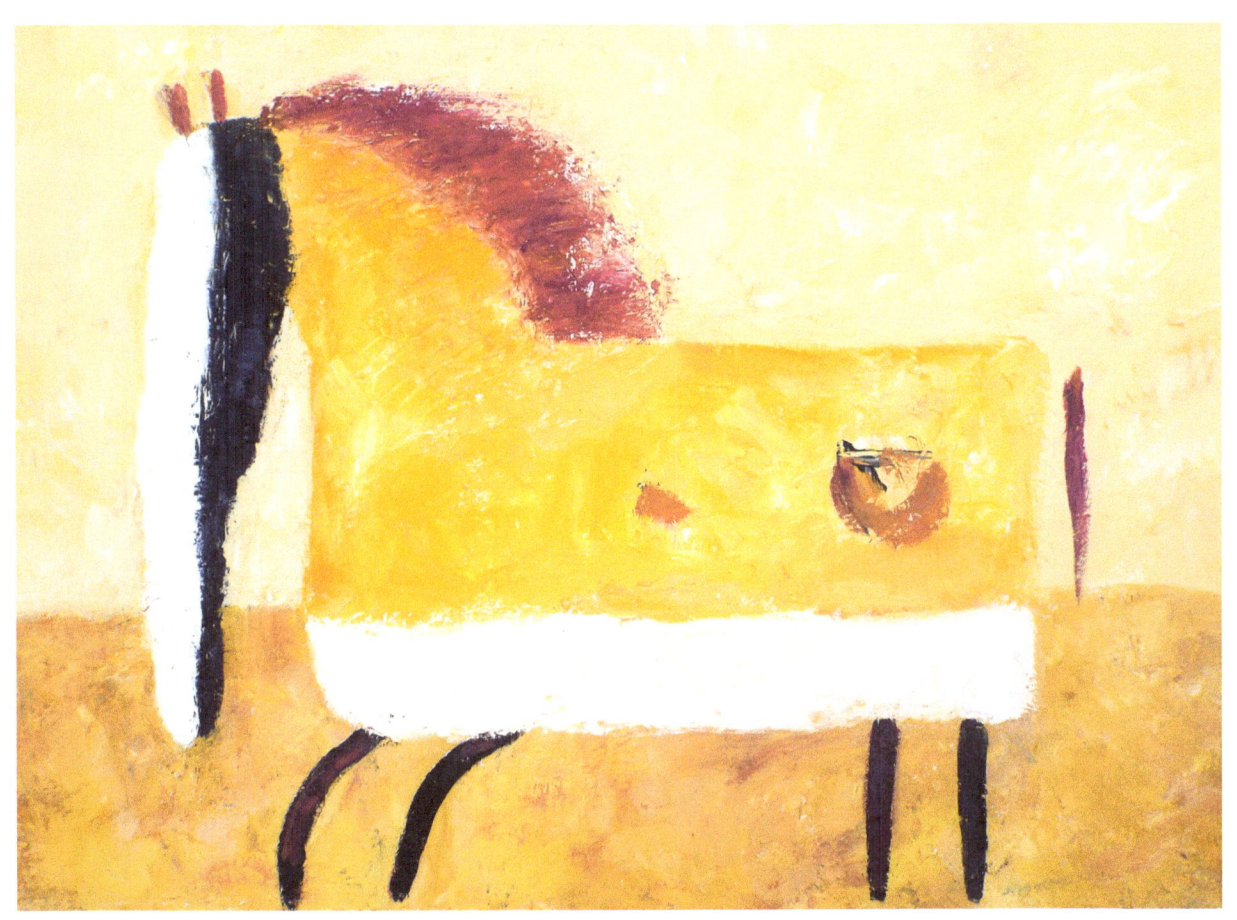

GREY SPOTTED HORSE IN PINK FIELD
Oil on canvas, 16 x 20 inches, 2017

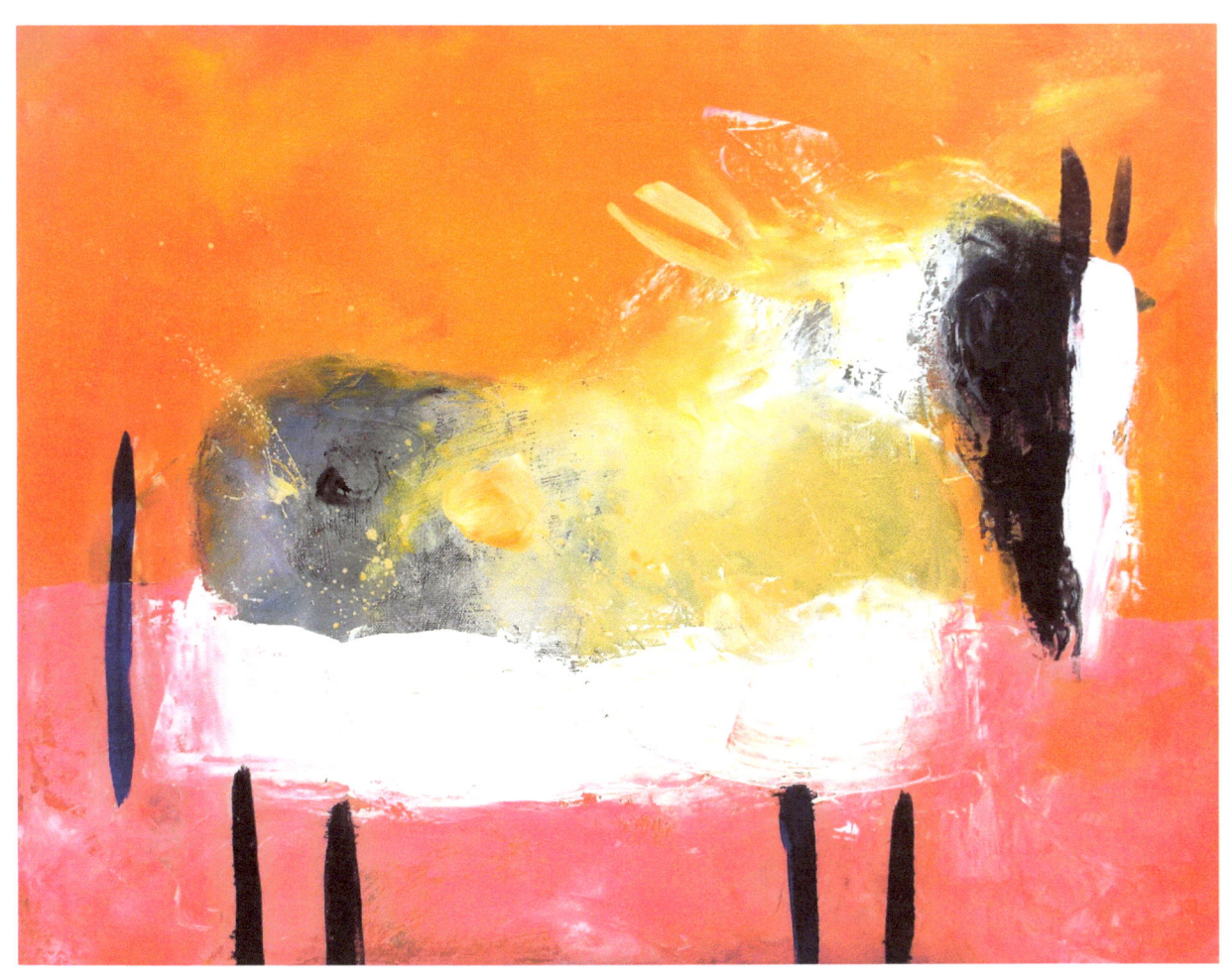

ANGKOR BISON WITH BELLS
Oil on paper, 30 x 34 inches, 2013

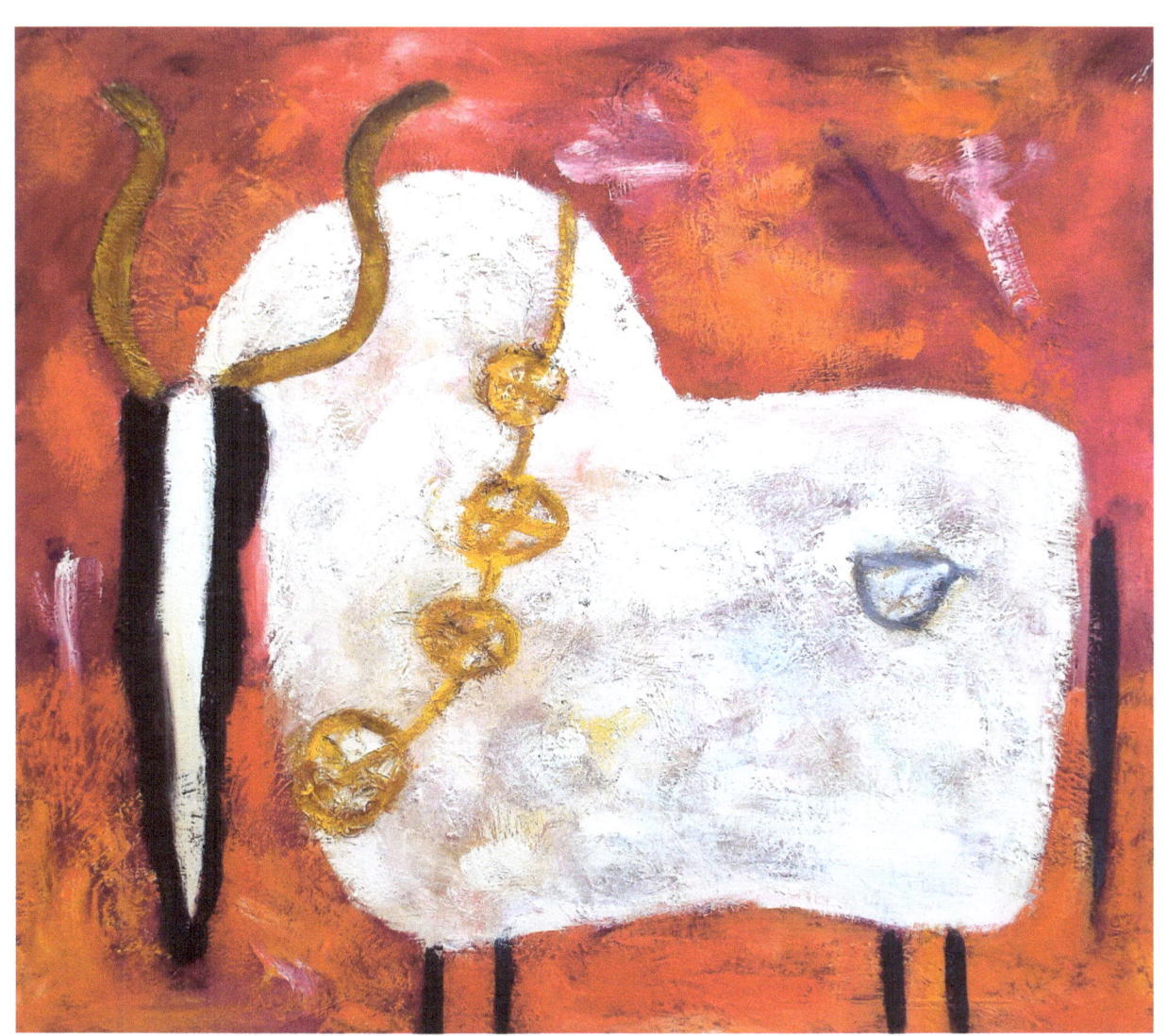

SPOTTED GOAT WITH SPIRAL HORNS
Oil on paper, 22 x 28 inches, 2017

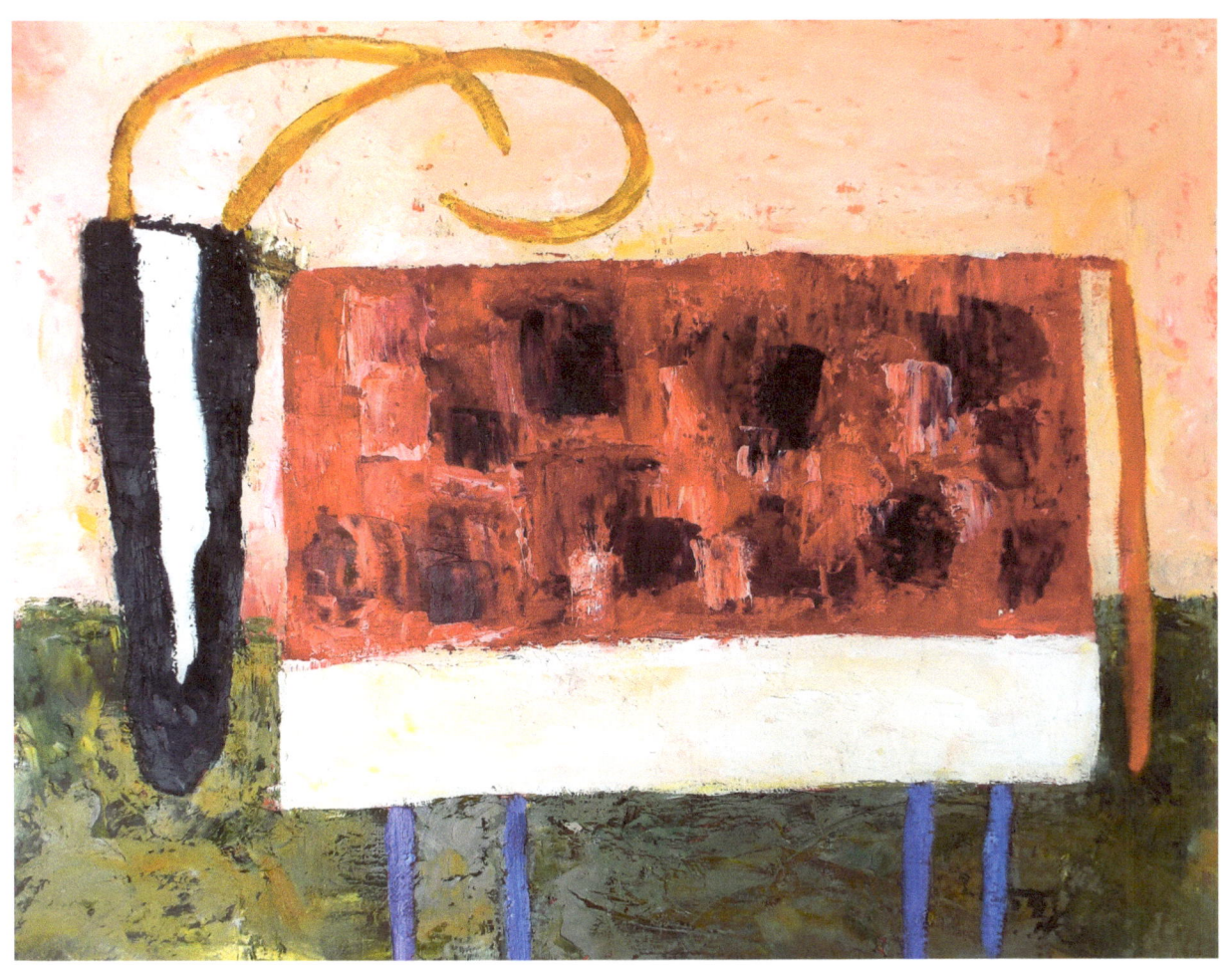

MONOTYPE AND WATERCOLORS

RECUMBENT HORSE WITH TURNING HEAD
Watercolor monotype with gouache, 12 x 9 inches, 2014

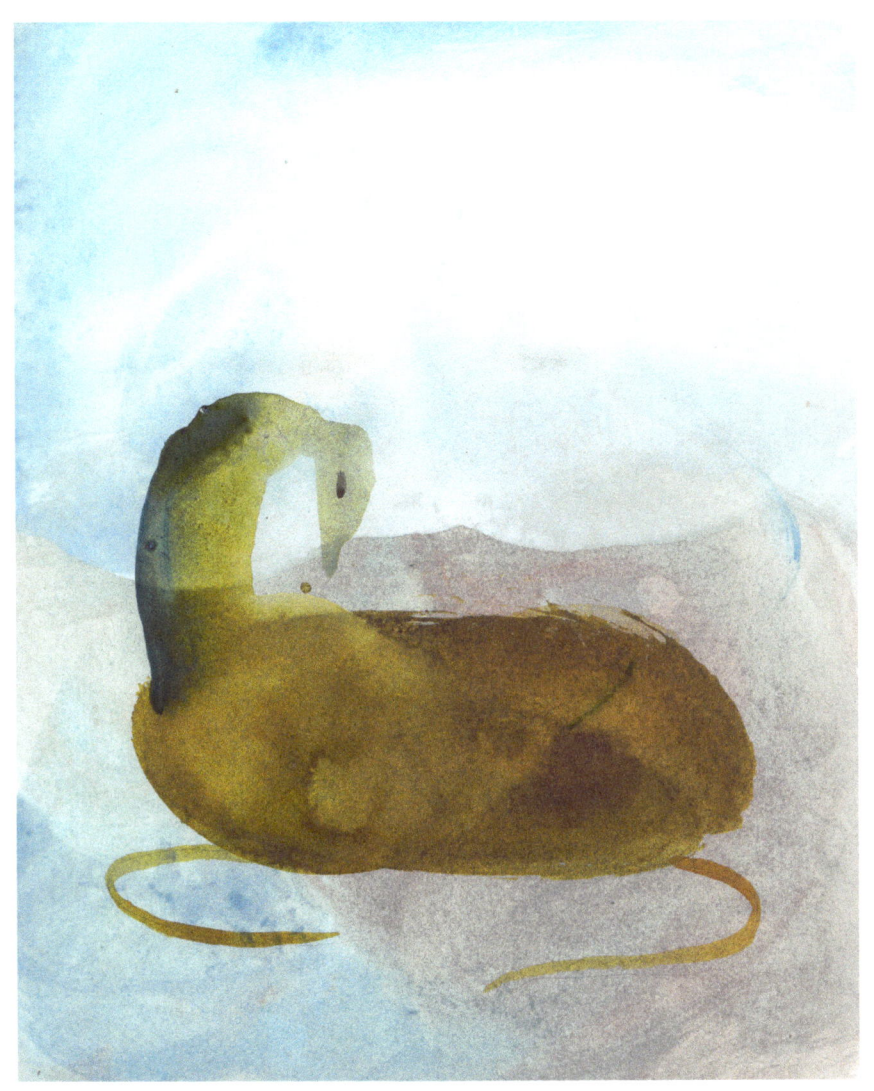

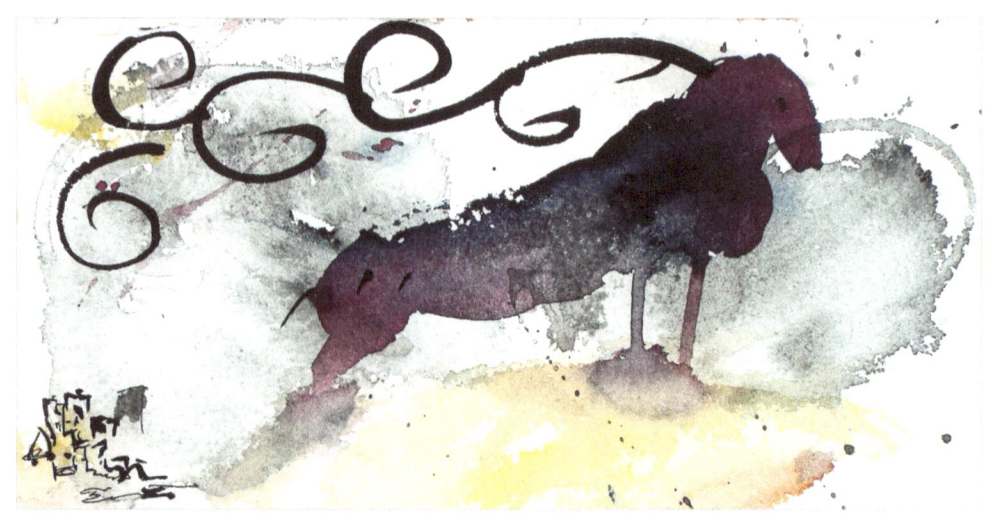

MARKHOR GOAT WITH SPIRAL HORNS
Watercolor and ink on paper, 4.5 x 9 inches, 2009

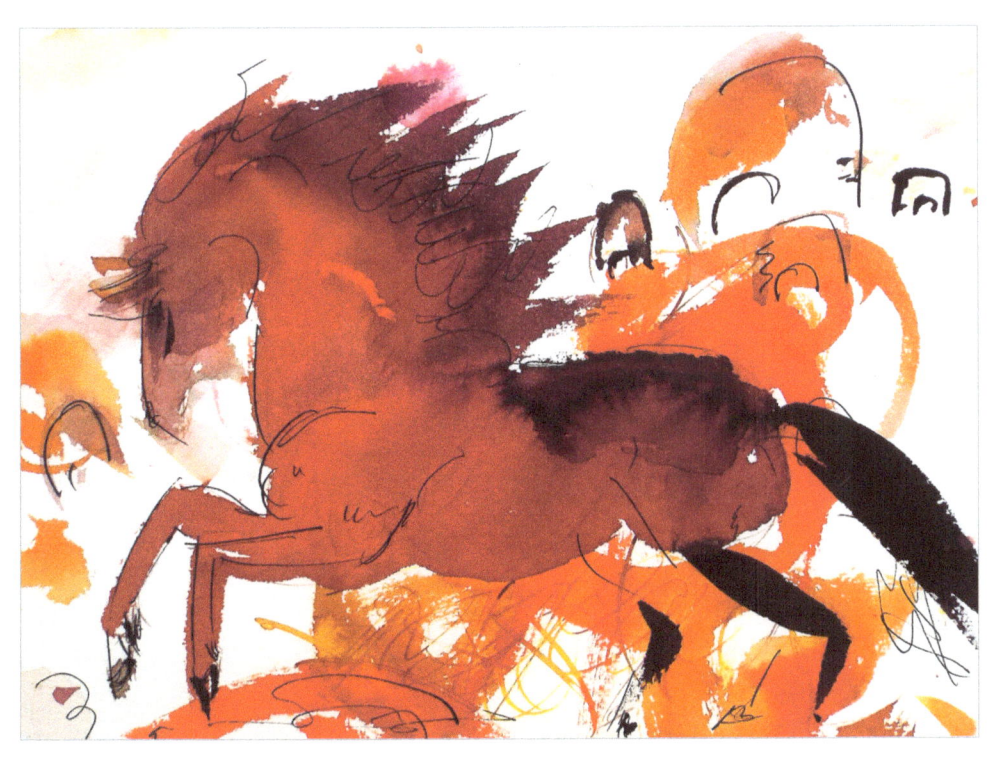

DUNHUANG HORSE
Watercolor and ink on paper, 6.25 x 8.75 inches, 2009

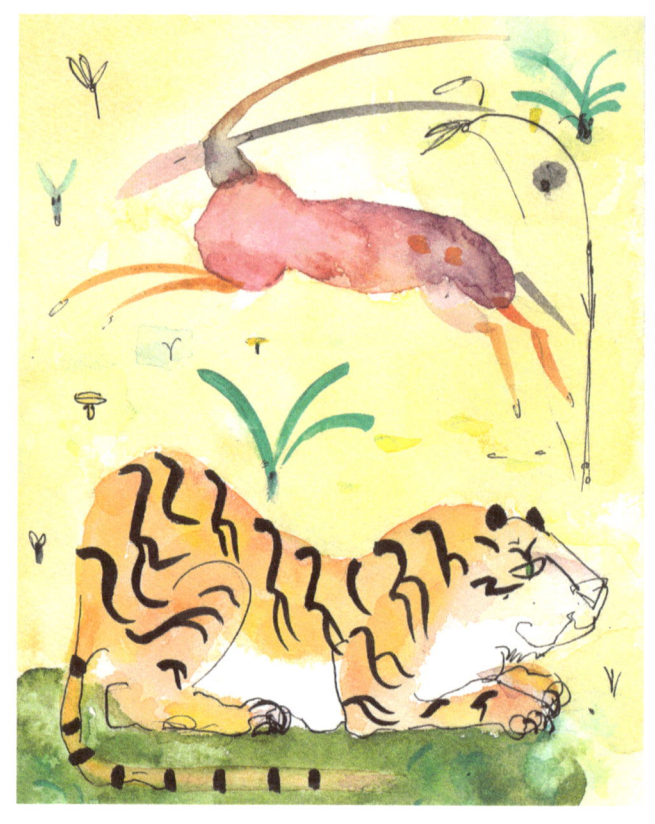

LEAPING DEER AND TIGER
Watercolor and ink on paper, 8.75 x 7 inches, 2009

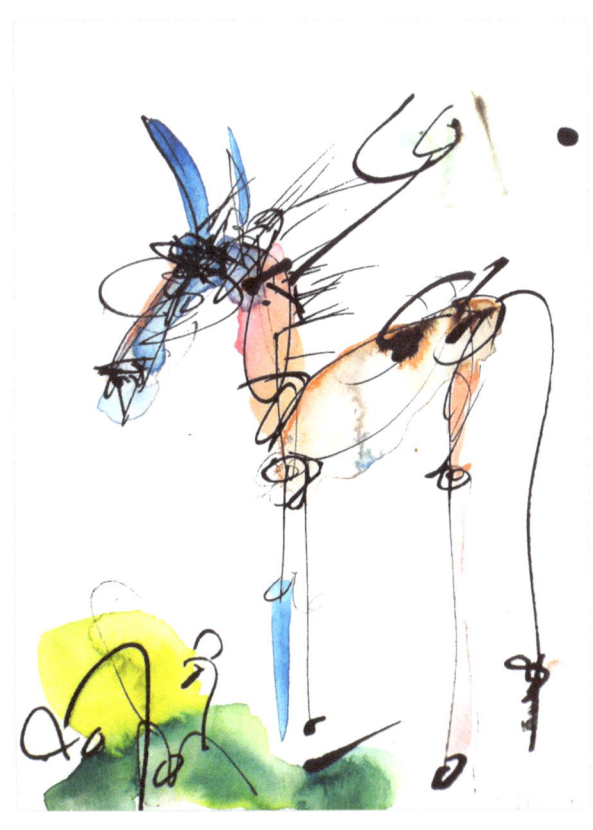

DONKEY
Watercolor and ink on paper, 7.5 x 5.5 inches, 2009

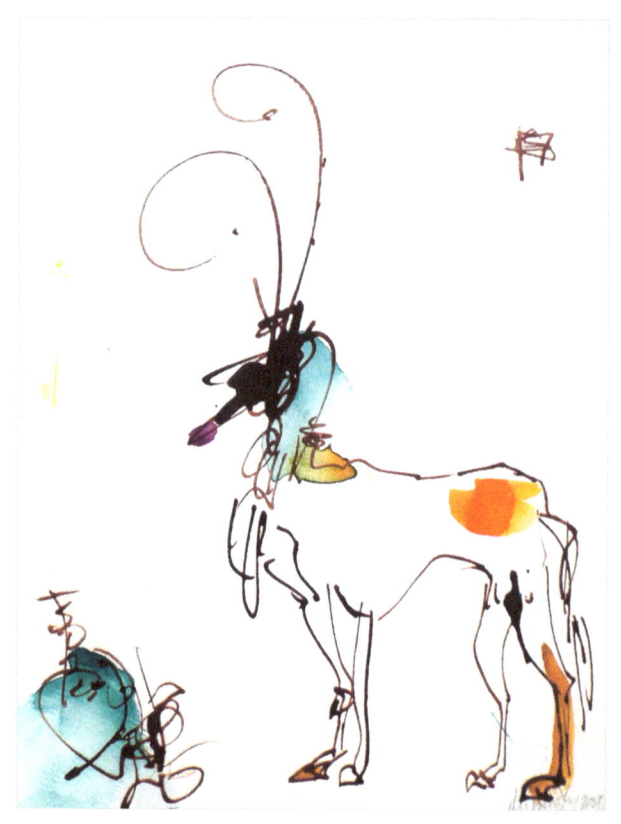

GOAT
Watercolor and ink on paper, 7.5 x 5.5 inches, 2009

RESUME

ONE-PERSON EXHIBITIONS (unless otherwise noted)

2016   "Journeys", Carter Burden Gallery, New York, NY (two-person show)
2008   "Mongolian Horses and Siberian Tigers", Cheryl Pelavin Fine Arts, New York, NY
        "Cambodian Flower Archaeology Monotypes", Cheryl Pelavin Fine Arts, New York, NY
2006   "Review: Cranes, Herons and Waterbirds", Cheryl Pelavin Fine Arts, New York, NY
        "Preview: Rainforests, Cloudforests and Pine", Cheryl Pelavin Fine Arts, New York, NY
        "Paintings", College of the Marshall Islands, Majuro, Republic of the Marshall Islands
2005   "The Crane Series", Ogilvie-Pertl Gallery, Chicago, IL
        "Riverbirds & Rainforests", The National Academies of Sciences, Washington, DC
        "Materia Medica", The Creative Center, New York, NY
2004   "The Crane & Heron Series", Cheryl Pelavin Fine Arts, New York, NY
        "Paintings by Valentina DuBasky", Friesen Fine Arts, Sun Valley, ID
        "Atlantic Flyway Project", Teaneck Creek Conservancy, Teaneck, NJ
2002   "New Paintings", Hodges Taylor Gallery, Charlotte, NC
        "New Paintings", Friesen Fine Arts, Sun Valley, ID
2001   "New Paintings", Silpakorn University Art Center Gallery, Bangkok, Thailand
        "Orchids and Fossils: New Landscape Paintings", Cheryl Pelavin Fine Arts, New York, NY
2000   "Ancient Futures: New Paintings & Monoprints", Cheryl Pelavin Fine Arts, New York, NY
        "Representation Debut," Friesen Fine Arts, Seattle, WA
        "Orchids on the Way to the Temple", Galerie Timothy Tew, Atlanta, GA
        "Through Bending Trees", Friesen Fine Arts, Sun Valley, ID
1998   "Memory and Light: New Paintings", Cheryl Pelavin Fine Arts, New York, NY
        "Materia Medica: New Monoprints", Cheryl Pelavin Fine Arts, New York, NY
1997   "Paintings", Hodges Taylor Gallery, Charlotte, NC
        "Landscape, Archaeology & Memory, Paintings, Sculpture & Monoprints 1985-97",
        University of North Carolina Gallery, Asheville, NC
1995   "Painting Retrospective", Rena Haveson Gallery, Pittsburgh, PA
        "Photographs", Gallery f32, Asheville, NC
1991   "New Paintings", Ruth Siegel Gallery, New York, NY
1990   "New Paintings", Ruth Siegel Gallery, New York, NY
1987   "Bronze Sculpture from the Caravan Series", Empire Bronze Art Gallery, LIC, NY
1986   "Paintings on Paper", Oscarsson-Siegeltuch Gallery, New York, NY
        "Paintings & Monotypes", Hodges Banks Gallery, Seattle, WA
1985   "Recent Paintings", van Straaten Gallery, Chicago, IL
        "Recent Paintings", Oscarsson Hood Gallery, New York, NY
        "Paintings from the Stag Series", Gloria Luria Gallery, Miami, FL
        "Monotypes", Jay Gallery, New York, NY
1984   "Recent Paintings", Susan Montazenos Gallery, Philadelphia, PA
1983   "Paintings from the Stag Series", Oscarsson Hood Gallery, New York, NY
        "Recent Paintings", Robert L. Kidd Gallery, Detroit, MI

1981   "Paintings on Paper", Oscarsson Hood Gallery, New York, NY
1980   "Paintings", Semaphore Gallery, New York, NY

SELECTED GROUP EXHIBITIONS

2017   "The Trace", Lichtundfire Gallery, New York, NY
2015   "Small Works", Carter Burden Gallery, New York, NY
          "True Monotypes", International Print Center New York, curated by Janice Oresman,
            New York, NY
          "Group Exhibition", McElwain Fine Arts, St Louis, MO
2014   "Shifting Ecologies", The Painting Center, New York, NY
          "Tandem Press Monoprints", Expo Chicago, Chicago, IL
          "Tandem Press Monoprints", IFPDA Print Fair, New York Armory, New York, NY
          "Tandem Press Monoprints", NYINK Art Fair, Miami Beach, FL
2013   "Tandem Press Monoprints", IFPDA Print Fair, New York Armory, New York, NY
          "Tandem Press Monoprints", NYINK Art Fair, Miami Beach, FL
2010   "Spring Prints", Cheryl Pelavin Fine Arts, New York, NY
2009   "Paintings", Friesen Fine Arts, Seattle, WA
          "Streetscapes", Landscapes, Still Lives, Jan Larsen Art, New York, NY
          "Art and Democracy", Gallery H, New York, NY
2008   "Friends", Cheryl Pelavin Fine Arts, New York, NY
          "From Different Horizons of Rock Shelter", Pang Mapha Archaeological Site, Thailand
          "From Different Horizons of Rock Shelter", National Gallery of Art, Bangkok, Thailand
          "Print Show", Cheryl Pelavin Fine Arts, New York, NY
2007   "25 Years of Printmaking at Cheryl Pelavin Fine Arts", Cheryl Pelavin Fine Arts, New York, NY
2006   "Alignment", Friesen Fine Art, Seattle, WA
          "Oil & Wax", Robert Roman Galleries, Scottsdale, AZ
          "Group Show", Ogilvie-Pertl Gallery, Chicago, IL
          "Art Scottsdale", Ogilvie-Pertl Gallery & Larsen Gallery, Scottsdale, AZ
          "Traveling Exhibition: Agent Orange: Consequence of War, a Call to Conscience",
            Marlboro College Gallery, Vermont; Brandeis University Gallery, Boston;
            George Washington University Gallery, Washington, DC
2005   "Oil & Wax: Chapter & Verse", Siano Gallery, Philadelphia, PA
2004   "Two Artists", Ogilvie-Pertl Gallery, Chicago, IL
          "The New Realism", Robert L. Kidd Gallery, Detroit, MI
          "Two Artists: Reflections of Cambodia", The Puffin Foundation, Teaneck, NJ
          "Returning the Brownfields of Teaneck Creek", Teaneck Creek Conservancy, Teaneck, NJ
          "Toxic Landscape", Long Beach Island Foundation of the Arts & Sciences, Love Ladies, NJ
          "Lower Manhattan Cultural Council Benefit", DKNY, New York, NY
          "Dealer's Choice", Robert L. Kidd Gallery, Detroit, MI

2003	Flora and Fauna: Manifestations", Cheryl Pelavin Fine Arts, New York, NY
	"American Artists", United States Embassy, Panama City, Panama
2002	"American Artists", United States Embassy, Riga, Latvia
	"American Artists", United States Embassy, Tallinn, Estonia
	"Two Artists", Friesen Fine Art, Seattle, WA
	"Fifteenth Anniversary Exhibition", Galerie Timothy Tew, Atlanta, GA
	"Affordable Art Fair", Cheryl Pelavin Fine Arts, New York, NY
	"The Head Show", Galerie Timothy Tew, Atlanta, GA
	"Reactions", Exit Art, New York, NY
	"Toxic Landscape: Artists Look at the Environment", Bibliotéca Nacional José Martí, Havana, Cuba
2001	"Group Exhibition", Friesen Fine Art, Seattle, WA
	"Group Exhibition", Norton Gallery, Seattle, WA
	"World Trade Center Benefit Exhibition", Cheryl Pelavin Fine Arts, New York, NY
2000	"Group Exhibition", Friesen Fine Art, Sun Valley, ID
1999	"American Artists", United States Embassy, Lima, Peru
	"American Artists", United States Embassy, Reykjavik, Iceland
	"American Artists", United States Embassy, Bangkok, Thailand
	"Sitting Pretty", Met Life Windows, New York, NY
	"Birdsong", Laurie Seeman Gallery, Nyack, NY
1998	"Visual Dialogues: 15 Women Artists", Robert Kidd Gallery, Detroit, MI
	"Nature/Culture", The New York Arts Exchange Show, New York, NY
	"Four Artists", Lone Star Park Gallery, Dallas, TX
	"Group Exhibition", Tower Air, curated by Jeannie Greenberg, New York, NY
1997	"Sizzle", Jeffrey Coploff Gallery, New York, NY
	"Group Exhibition", Hillwood Museum, Chattanooga, TN
	"Art of Hearts", Nora Haime Gallery & the National Academy of Design, New York, NY
	"Group Exhibition", Hodges Taylor Gallery, Charlotte, NC
	"The National Horse Show", Robert Kidd Gallery, Detroit, MI
1996	"Partners in Printmaking: Works from Solo Impressions", National Museum of Women in the Arts, Washington, DC
	"Painting Exhibition", Hillwood Museum, Long Island University, NY
	"Three Photographers", June Kelly Gallery, New York, NY
	"American Artists", United States Embassy, Muscat, Oman
	"Recent Monotype Editions", Pelavin Editions, New York, NY
	"Group Exhibition", Robert L. Kidd Gallery, Detroit, MI
1995	"American Artists", United States Embassy, Amman, Jordan
	"Inaugural Exhibition", Michele Bigue Gallery, Fort Lauderdale, FL
1994	"American Artists", United States Embassy, Oslo, Norway
	"Group Exhibition", ES Painting Space, New York, NY
1993	"Animal Imagery", Champion Paper, curated by Janice Oresman, Hartfield, CT

1992	"34 Raumes", Documenta, Berlin, Germany
	"Printmaking from the Permanent Collection", Jane Voorhees Zimmerli Art Museum, Rutgers University, NJ
	"Works on Paper from Pelavin Editions", The Armory Show, New York, NY
1991	"Works on Paper", Champion Paper, Stanford, CT
1990	"Intaglio Printing in the 1980's", Jane Voorhees Zimmerli Art Museum, Rutgers University, New Brunswick, NJ
	"Women in Print", Traveling museum exhibition, National Museum of Women in the Arts, Washington, DC
	"Menagerie", General Electric Company Headquarters, curated by MOMA Advisory Services, CT
1989	"Surface Printing in the 1980's", Jane Voorhees Zimmerli Art Museum, Rutgers University, New Brunswick, NJ
	"Creatures", Benson Gallery, Bridgehampton, NY
1988	"Three Sculptors Working in Bronze", Gallerie Helene Grubair, Miami, FL
1987	"Group Show", Albright Knox Museum, Buffalo, NY
1986	"Monotypes by Gallery Artists", Oscarsson-Siegeltuch Gallery, New York, NY
	"Paintings", van Straaten Gallery, Chicago, IL
	"Inaugural Exhibition", Group Show, Oscarsson-Siegeltuch Gallery, New York, NY
	"Homage to Ana Mendieta", Zeus Trabia Gallery, New York, NY
	"Monotypes", Jay Gallery, New York, NY
1985	"Art of the 70's & 80's", Aldrich Museum of Contemporary Art, Ridgefield, CT
	"1985 Invitational Quinquennial Exhibition", Oscarsson Hood Gallery, New York, NY
	"Selections from the Jane Voorhees Zimmerli Art Museum", The Grolier Club, New York, NY
	"Chicago Art Expo", Oscarsson Hood Gallery, Chicago, IL
	"Pelavin Editions 1985", Jay Gallery, New York, NY
	"Monotypes and Works on Paper", Robert L. Kidd Gallery, Detroit, MI
	"Animals: Contemporary Visions", Robert L. Kidd Gallery, Detroit, MI
	"The Animal Within", Jay Gallery, New York, NY
	"Young Printmakers", Roger Ramsey Gallery, Chicago, IL
	"Two Artists", Peri Renneth Gallery, West Hampton, NY
1984	"Painting Invitational", Robeson Center Gallery, Rutgers University, New Brunswick, NJ
	"Situations", Jamaica Arts Center, The Newark Museum Collection, Newark, NJ
	"Review/Preview", Oscarsson Hood Gallery, New York, NY
	"Works on Paper", Wolff Gallery, New York, NY
	"8 at 84", Robert Feldman Gallery, New York, NY
	"Works on Paper", Barbara Greene Gallery, Miami, FL
	"Ringing in the New", Jay Gallery, New York, NY
1983	"New Acquisitions", Newark Museum, Newark, NJ
	"Art on Paper", Weatherspoon Museum, Greensboro, NC
	"Group Exhibition", Oscarsson Hood Gallery, New York, NY

"Works on Paper", Frumpkin Struve Gallery, Chicago, IL
"Group Show", Albright Knox Museum, Buffalo, NY
1982   "Group Show", Albright Knox Museum, Buffalo, NY
"New Acquisitions", Alternative Museum, New York, NY
"Mixed Bag", Alternative Museum, New York, NY
"Group Exhibition", McNay Art Institute, Collectors Gallery VI, Austin, TX
"Works on Paper", Roger Ramsey Gallery, Chicago, IL
"Group Exhibition", Oscarsson Hood Gallery, New York, NY
1981   "New Acquisitions", Aldrich Museum of Contemporary Art, CT
"Nine Artists Invited", Meisal Gallery, New York, NY
"Group Exhibition", Semaphore Gallery, New York, NY
"The Working Process", O.I.A. Exhibition, New York, NY
"Group Exhibition", Newcomber Westreich Gallery, Washington, DC
1980   "Small Works", 80 Gallery, Washington Square East, New York, NY
"Group Show," Race Gallery, Philadelphia, PA
"4 Artists", Soho Center for Visual Artists, New York, NY
"Betty Parsons at Robert L. Kidd Gallery", Robert L. Kidd Gallery, Detroit, MI

MUSEUM COLLECTIONS

Alternative Museum, New York, NY
Herbert F. Johnson Museum, Cornell University, Ithaca, NY
National Museum of Women in the Arts, Washington, DC
Newark Museum, Newark, NJ
Orlando Museum of Art, Orlando, FL
Seattle Art Museum, Seattle, WA
Jane Voorhees Zimmerli Art Museum, Rutgers, NJ
Xianghai Museum, Xianghai Nature Reserve, Xianghai, China

SELECTED PUBLIC COLLECTIONS

Agrace Hospice Care, Madison, WI
Architectural Arts, Inc, Dallas, TX
Banca della Suizzeria Italiana, NY, NY
Bank Boston, Boston, MA
Barron & Budd, NY, NY

Chase Manhattan Bank, NY, NY
Chemical Bank, NY, NY
Citibank International, Miami, FL
Denrich Leasing Company, Miami, FL
Echo Lab, MN
Carey Ellis Company, MN
Ernst & Young, NY, NY
Evergreen Asset & Management Corporation, NY, NY
Federal Reserve Bank, Chicago, IL
First National Bank, Boston, MA
Fuzhou International Center, Fuzhou, China
General Instruments, NY, NY
General Mills, Inc, Minneapolis, MN
Goldman-Sachs, NY, NY
Gruntal, NY, NY
Henson & Effron, St. Paul, MN
Hospital Corporation of North America, Nashville, TN
IBM Collection, Los Angeles, CA
Indiana National Bank, Boston, TX
International Data Group, Boston, MA
Kempner Insurance Company, NY, NY
King Investment Advisor, Inc, Houston, TX
Lang Communications, NY, NY
Library of Congress (Exit Art Reactions Exhibition), Washington, DC
Sidney Lewis Collection, Richmond, VA
Martin Margulies Collection, Miami, FL
Mayo Clinic, Rochester, MN
McDonalds Corporation, Oak Brook, IL
The Mercer Company, NY, NY
J. P. Morgan & Company, NY, NY
Morgan Guarantee, NY, NY
Nutter, McClennan & Fish, Boston, MA
Palm Hills Hotel, Okinawa, Japan
Peat, Marwich, Mitchell & Co, Montvale, NJ
Pew Charitable Trust, Philadelphia, Pa
Pfizer Pharmaceuticals, Inc, NY, NY
Polsinelli Collection, Los Angeles, CA
Prudential Life Insurance Company, Rockefeller Center, NY, NY
Quad Graphics, West Allis, IL
Quaker Oats, Chicago, IL

Randolph & Tate Associates, NY, NY
Reich & Tang, NY, NY
Simpson, Thacher, Bartlett, NY, NY
Skadden, Arps, Slate, Meagher & Flom, NY, NY
Solomon Equities, Inc, NY, NY
Tower Air, NY, NY
United States Department of State, Washington, DC
Vinson Elkins, Houston, TX
Wachovia, Charlotte, NC
E.M. Warburg Pincus, NY, NY
WFAE National Public Radio, Charlotte, NC
C. Wright Design, Mill Valley, CA
Zale Corporation, Dallas, TX
Zelle & Larson, St. Paul, MNWachovia, Charlotte, NC
E.M. Warburg Pincus, New York, NY
WFAE National Public Radio, Charlotte, NC
C. Wright Design, Mill Valley, CA
Zale Corporation, Dallas, TX
Zelle & Larson, St. Paul, MN

GRANTS

2016   Fulbright Specialist Program, India

2006   Visiting Artist Grant, Pang Mapha Highland Archaeology Project, Thailand

2003   Earthwork Installation Grant, Atlantic Flyway Project, Teaneck Creek Conservancy

2002   American Artists Abroad, Art in Ambassies Program Grant, US Department of State, Riga, Latvia
        American Artists Abroad, Art in Ambassies Program Grant, US Department of State, Tallinn, Estonia
        The Puffin Foundation Grant, paintings and photographs

2001   United States Embassy Visiting Artist Grant, Bangkok, Thailand

1999   Pollock Krasner Foundation

1986   Pollock Krasner Foundation

1984   Ariana Foundation for the Arts

TELEVISION FEATURES

WETA Public Television   AROUND TOWN/ BEST BETS WITH JANICE GOODMAN   5 August, 2005
Review by Janice Goodman
One-person exhibition of "Riverbirds & Rainforests" at the National Academy of Sciences Gallery, Washington, DC

Apsara Television   9 June, 2007
Cambodian Journal: One-person exhibition at the Java Arts, Phnom Penh, Cambodia

TELEVISION OF THAILAND CHANNEL 11   July, 2001
Ancient Futures: One-person exhibition, Silpakorn Gallery, Silpakorn Universitiy, Bangkok, Thailand

REVIEWS (of one-person exhibitions)

2008   ABSOLUTEARTS.COM: INDEPTH ART NEWS   "Mongolian Horses and Siberian
        Tigers-New Paintings on Paper and Canvas"   October 23, 2008
        One-person exhibition at Cheryl Pelavin Fine Arts, New York, NY
        Color Reproduction: *Crouching Tiger,* 2008

2006   THE NEW YORKER   17 April, 2006
        Review by Martha Schwendener
        One-person exhibition at Cheryl Pelavin Fine Arts, New York, NY

2005   THE WASHINGTON DIPLOMAT   "Larger Than Life: DuBasky's Oversize Work
        Focuses on Animal, Plant Life Along Silk Road"   October, 2005
        Review by Venessa LaFaso
        One-person exhibition at the National Academy of Sciences Gallery, Washington, DC
        Color reproductions: *Gray Bird and Branches,* 2005, *Riverbirds, Fossils and Reeds,* 2005
        and *Mountain Site,* 2003

        THE EXAMINER   29 October, 2005
        Review by Robin Tierney
        One-person exhibition at National Academy of Sciences Gallery, Washington, DC
        Color Reproduction: *Red Bird & Reeds,* 2005

2001   TRIBECA TRIBUNE   Vol. 8, No. 4, December, 2001
        Review by Jeanne C. Wilkinson
        One-person exhibition at Cheryl Pelavin Fine Arts, New York, NY
        Color Reproduction: *Forest Site Wat Phimai,* 2001

2000   THE NEW YORK TIMES   4 February, 2000
        Review by Ken Johnson
        One-person exhibition at Cheryl Pelavin Fine Arts, New York, NY

        REVIEW   January, 2000
        Review by Joel Silverstein
        One-person exhibition at Cheryl Pelavin Fine Arts, New York, NY

        IDAHO MOUNTAIN EXPRESS, ARTS & EVENTS, pC-2   2 August, 2000
        Anon.
        One-person exhibition at Andria Friesen Fine Arts, Seattle, WA
        Color Reproduction: *Forest Site with Spotted Stag,* 2000

1999   ART IN AMERICA   January, 1999
        Review by Gerrit Henry
        One-person exhibition at Cheryl Pelavin Fine Arts, New York, NY
        Color Reproduction: *Syntax,* 1998

1997   CHARLOTTE NEWSSTAND, ARTS & ENTERTAINMENT   1 November, 1997
        Review by Jane Grau
        One-person exhibition at Hodges Taylor Gallery, Charlotte, NC
        Color Reproduction: *Red Spotted Horse,* 1997

1991   ARTFORUM   December, 1991
        Review by Ronny Cohen
        One-person exhibition at Ruth Siegel Gallery, New York, NY
        Color Reproduction: *Indonesia,* 1991

1986   ART IN AMERICA   April, 1986
        Review by Gerrit Henry
        One-person exhibition at Oscarsson-Hood Gallery, New York, NY
        Reproduction: *Primate,* 1986

        THE WEEKLY   "Modern Day Cave Painting"   Vol. 11, No. 25   18 June, 1986
        Review by Doen Broelley
        One-person exhibition at Hodges Banks Gallery, Seattle, WA
        Color Reproduction: *Sienna Stag,* 1984

1985   GALLERY GUIDE   December, 1985
        Anon.
        One-person exhibition at Oscarsson-Hood Gallery, New York, NY
        Reproduction: *Rough Beast,* 1984

MIAMI NEWS, MIAMI ART SCENE   April, 1985
Review by Paula Harper
One-person exhibition at Gloria Luria Gallery, Miami, FL

WOMEN ARTISTS NEWS   "Prehistory to Post Modernism"   Vol. 9, No. 2, Winter, 1983-4
Review by John Arthur Shanks
One-person exhibition at Oscarsson-Hood Gallery, New York, NY
Reproduction: *Fallow Deer in Bracken,* 1983

1983   ARTS MAGAZINE   1983
Review by William Zimmer
One-person exhibition at Oscarsson-Hood Gallery, New York, NY
Reproduction: *Amber Stag,* 1983

1981   ARTS MAGAZINE   Vol. 55, No. 6   1981
Review by Addison Parks
One-person exhibition at Semaphore Gallery, New York, NY
Color Reproduction: *Split Cow,* 1981

ARTSPEAK   Vol. 2, No. 9   1981
Review by William Pellicone
One-person exhibition at Semaphore Gallery, New York, NY
Reproduction: *Split Cow,* 1981

WOMEN ARTISTS NEWS   Winter/Spring, 1981
Review by John Arthur Shanks
One-person exhibition at Semaphore Gallery, New York, NY
Color Reproduction: *Split Cow,* 1981

FEATURE ARTICLES

2006   THE NEW YORK SUN, ON THE TOWN   "Rain Clouds: Valentina DuBasky at
Cheryl Pelavin Fine Arts"   18 May, 2006, p12
Anon.
Color Reproduction: *Riverbank Late Afternoon,* 2006

2003   ART & ANTIQUES   "Reimagining the Landscape: Contemporary Painters Bring Fresh Ideas
and Techniques to a Classic Art Form"   Vol. 26, No. 10, October, 2003, p 71
Article by Edward M. Gomez
Color Reproduction: *Open Forest,* 2001

MAKSLA PLUS, KULTURAS ZURNALS   "Amerikas maksla Riga"   Vol. 1, No. 33, February/ March, 2003, pgs 11 & 13
Article by Gundega Cebere
Color Reproduction: *Heron,* 1995 and *Heron, Warbler and Milkweed,* 1991

STATE MAGAZINE   "The Art of Visual Diplomacy"   No. 464, January, 2003, pgs 1 and 13
Article by Elizabeth Ash

2002   ARCHITECTURE AND DESIGN IN THE BALTICS   "Old Birds Under One Roof"   No. 5
Riga, Latvia, October, 2002, pgs 11 and 25
Article by Irina Osadchaja
Color reproductions: *Heron,* 1995 and *Heron, Warbler and Milkweed,* 1991

2000   SEATTLE WOOD RIVER JOURNAL   "Western Explorers Meet Explorations on Canvas and Film"   2 August, 2000, p1
Artcle by Susan Bailey
Color Reproduction: *Forest Site with River & Orchids,* 2000

SUN VALLEY ART   "Painting/ Profile: Modern Landscape Painting"   Vol. 6, Nos. 8 & 9
February-March, 2000
Article by Meagan Stasz
Color reproductions: *Forest Site with Orchids & Wild Grass,* 2000 and
Forest Canopy & Botanicas, 2000

1986   ARTS MAGAZINE   "Hudson River Editions, Pelavin Editions-A Report Back from the Other World of Printmaking"   November, 1986, p42
Article by Timothy Cohrs
Color Reproduction: *Stag/Red Meander,* 1985

1981   THE WASHINGTON POST "Seventh Street Galleries Celebrate Reopening"   19 September. 1981
Article by Joseph Mclellan

REPRODUCTIONS (of paintings in publications)

2006   LUXE MAGAZINE, INTERIORS + DESIGN PACIFIC NORTHWEST EDITION   "Tall Order"
Issue 1, Vol. 8, Winter, 2010, p178
Article by Linda Hayes
Color Reproduction: *River Fragments Grey Bird,* 1990

THE LAKEVILLE JOURNAL   10 August, 2006, pC12
Reproduction: *Eurasian Steppe Horse,* 2004

2002   SOUTHERN VOICE Atlanta   11 October, 2002
        Article by Christopher Seely
        Color Reproduction: *Yellow Bird in Grey Field*   2002

2000   IDAHO MOUNTAIN EXPRESS, ARTS & EVENTS SUN VALLEY   2 August, 2000
        Color Reproduction: *Forest Site with Spotted Stag,* 2000

1999   THE SCIENCES MAGAZINE   Volume 39, No. 4, p5, July/August 1999
        Color Reproduction: *Pond Site,* 1999

1997   CAROLINA ARTS   "Hodges Taylor Gallery is Moving"   Vol. 1, No. 9, 1997, p19
        Color Reproduction: *Red Spotted Horse,* 1997

        SOUTHERN ACCENTS Charlotte   1997
        Color Reproduction: *Red Horse/ Split,* 1997

1992   CHRISTIAN SCIENCE MONITOR   23 November, 1992
        Color Reproduction: *Heron Cove,* 1990

1991   THE MENNIGER PERSPECTIVE   Issue No. 3, 1991
        Color Reproduction: *Eastern Quarter,* 1991

990   MS MAGAZINE poster publication
        Color Reproduction: *Heron Cove,* 1990

1988   THE POLLOCK KRASNER FOUNDATION ANNUAL REPORT   1987-1988
        Reproduction: *Strata,* 1984

        LEGACY FOUNDATION
        Color cover Reproduction: *Good Medicine,* monoprint and chine colle, 1996

1985   THE SCIENCES MAGAZINE   "The Ancestor that Wasn't"   March/April, 1985, p46
        Color Reproduction: *Back to Back,* 1984

1983   THE NEWARK MUSEUM ANNUAL REPORT
        Reproduction: *Bucks Country,* 1983

1980   MAENAD MAGAZINE
        Color cover Reproduction: *Spotted Bison,* and 4 paintings, 1980

REVIEWS (of international exhibitions)

2007   THE CAMBODIA DAILY   "Back to Basics: Two Artists' Return to Drawing"   Issue 483, June, 2007
        Review by Michelle Vachon
        Color reproductions: *Crossing the Street in Hanoi,* 1994 and *Resting Soldier,* 1994

ASIA LIFE   "Cambodian Journal: Human resilience and the strong Cambodian spirit are themes that artist Valentina DuBasky explores in her new exhibition"
Review by Liz Ledden, 2007

2002   STATE MAGAZINE   "In the News: Artist and Their Art Go Abroad"   No. 463
December, 2002, p5
Color Reproduction: *Heron, Warbler and Milkweed,* 1991

BANGKOK POST   "Ancient Futures: Cave-wall Landscape Paintings"   22 June 2001, p1
Color reproductions: *Forest Site with Orchids & Bending Trees,* 2000

2001   NAEW NA   "Ancient Futures: New Cave-Wall Landscape by Valentina DuBasky"   June, 2001

2000   THE NATION   "New and Old"   Bangkok, Thailand   16 July, 2001
Color reproductions: *Forest Site with Orchids & Bending Trees,* 2000

SIAM RATH   "Ancient Futures"   21 June, 2001
Color reproductions: *Forest Site with Orchids & Bending Trees,* 2000 & *Forest Floor with Orchids,* 2000

BANGKOK POST   "Ancient Futures: Cave-wall Landscape Paintings"   2000
Color Reproduction: *Forest Site with Stag & Bird,* 2000

REVIEWS (of print publications)

2014   ART IN PRINT   "Selected New Editions"   March-April, 2014
Anon.
Color Reproduction: *Cliff Site with Red Heron,* monoprint, 2013

JOURNAL OF THE PRINT WORLD   "New Editions"   April/May/June, 2014
Anon.
Color Reproduction: *Amber Birds with Indigo Mountain,* 2013

2001   IN NEW YORK/ ECLECTIC COLLECTOR   July, 2008
Review by Erin Szeto-Chan
Color Reproduction: *Tiger Orchid/ Sri Lanka,* monoprint, 2001

1992   TWENTY-FIRST CENTURY PRINTS   August, 1992
Review by Meri Marimo
Color Reproduction: *River Edge,* monoprint, 1990

1988   PRINT NEWS: INTERNATIONAL JOURNAL OF CONTEMPORARY PRINTS
Vol. 8, No. 2, Spring, 1988   ssAnon.
Color Reproduction: *Ragtime Hart,* monoprint,1985

1986   WEST SIDE SPIRIT/ ARTS & ENTERTAINMENT   "Ancient Art Comes Alive"   14 July, 1986
Review by Tom Beller
Color Reproductions: *Leaping Brindled Stag,* 1984 and *Ragtime Hart,* 1984

1984   ARTNEWS "New Editions"   April, 1984
Review by Ronny Cohen
Color Reproduction: *Dune Horse/Starry Night,* lithograph, 1984

THE PRINT COLLECTORS NEWSLETTER   Vol. 15, No. 3, July-August, 1984
Anon.
Color Reproductions: *Claret Stag in Plum Field,* 1984; *Leaping Brindled Stag,* etchings, 1984

1983   THE PRINT COLLECTORS NEWSLETTER   Vol. 14, No. 5
Anon.
Color Reproduction: *Dune Horse/Starry Night,* 1983

REVIEWS (of group exhibitions)

2000   TRIBUNE/REVIEW   "Pair of Shows Comment on Environmental Issues Facing Our Nation and the World"   16 November, 2001
Review by Kurt Shaw

1988   THE MIAMI NEWS   "Sculpture is the focus of Gallery Show"   3 June, 1988
Review by Leslie Judd Ahlander
Reproduction: *Standing Camel,* 1988

1985   ARTNEWS   "Group Show: Wolff Gallery"   January, 1985
Review by Sarah Cecil

1983   DETROIT FREE PRESS   November, 1983
Review by Marsha Miro
Detroit News, November, 1983

1981   WHERE MAGAZINE   August, 1981
Anon.

1980   THE VILLAGE VOICE   "Reports from the Front"   Vol. 25, No. 7
Review by Kay Larsen

THE VILLAGE VOICE   1980
Review by Carrie Rickey

EXHIBITION CATALOGS

2017 THE TRACE
Essay by Jonathan Goodman
Color reproduction: *Winged Horse and Figure,* 2017

2016 THE JOURNEY OF THE RED HORSE: HORSE AND STAG PAINTINGS
BY VALENTINA DUBASKY
Published by Abingdon Square Publishing
Color reproductions: 13 color plates

2015 KINETIV: HIGHLIGHTS FROM THE POLSINELLI ART COLLECTION
Edited by Mary Walsh
Published by Polsinelli
Color reproduction: *Amber Birds with Indigo Montain,* Monotype, 2013

2014 TANDEM PRESS: FINE CONTEMPORARY PRINTS
MONOTYPES AND LITHOGRAPH WITH ENCAUSTIC AND COLLAGE
BY VALENTINA DUBASKY
Published by Tandem Press
Color Reproductions: 15 color plates

2008 FROM [DIFFERENT] HORIZONS OF ROCKSHELTER
Exhibition catalog essay by Rasmi Shoocongdej
Published by Silpakorn University Press, Bangkok, Thailand
Color reproductions: 6 paintings from the Pang Mapha Highland Archaeology Project

2005 RIVERBIRDS AND RAINFOREST PAINTINGS BY VALENTINA DUBASKY AT
THE NATIONAL ACADEMIES OF SCIENCES
Exhibition catalog essay by Cynthia Nadelman; **Forward** by JD Talasek
Published by the National Academies of Sciences, Washington, DC
Color reproductions: 11 color plates

2003 UNITED STATES EMBASSY PANAMA: ARTS IN EMBASSY PROGRAM, images: pgs 6 and 7
Exhibition catalog essay by United States Ambassador Linda E. Watt
Printed by the United States Department of State
Color reproductions: *Untitled,* 1998, *Shore Site,* 1991 and *Rainforest,* 1999

2002 ART IN EMBASSIES EXHIBITION AT THE RESIDENCE OF THE AMERICAN AMBASSADOR
RIGA, LATVIA
Exhibition catalog essay by United States Ambassador Brian E. Carlson
Printed by the United States Department of State
Color reproductions: *Heron, Warbler and Milkweed,* 1991 (cover) and *Heron,* 1995

TOXIC LANDSCAPES: ARTISTS EXAMINE THE ENVIRONMENT, image: p20
Printed by the Puffin Foundation
Reproduction: *Tragic Harvest,* 1991

2001 FORESTS, ORCHIDS & FOSSILSBY VALENTINA DUBASKY   7 November, 2001
Exhibition catalog essay by Gerrit Henry
Color reproductions: 9 color plates

1999 OIL & WAX: CHAPTER & VERSE
Color Reproduction: *Spotted Horse,* 1999

1998 AMERICAN ARTISTS AT AMERICAN AMBASSADOR'S RESIDENCES
MUSCAT, SULTANATE OF OMAN, images: p14
Exhibition catalog essay by United States Ambassador Frances D. Cook
Printed by United States Department of State
Color Reproduction: *Heron Cove,* 1990

1990 PRESSWORK: THE ART OF WOMEN PRINTMAKERS
Exhibition catalog essays by Eleanor Heartney and Trudy Hanson
Printed by Lang Publications, 1990
Color Reproduction: *Heron Cove,* 1990

1987 THE NEW YORK ART REVIEW
Printed by the American References Publishing Corporation, Chicago, IL

THE CARAVAN SERIES
SCULPTURE BY VALENTINA DUBASKY
Reproductions: 10 plates

1985 INTAGLIO PRINTING IN THE 1980'S
Printed by the Jane Voorhees Zimmerli Art Museum

1984 RUTGERS ARCHIVES FOR PRINTMAKING STUDIOS, CATALOG OF ACQUISITIONS,
1985-1987
Printed by the Jane Voorhees Zimmerli Art Museum, Rutgers University
Reproductions: *Red Stag Diptych,* 1984, *Leaping Brindled Stag,* 1984, *Claret Stag in Plum
Field,* 1984, *Small Stag Series,* 1984, and *Gray Stag/ Ochre Field,* 1984

SURFACE PRINTING IN THE 1980'S; LITHOGRAPHS, SCREENPRINTS & MONOPRINTS
FROM THE RUTGERS ARCHIVES FOR PRINTMAKING STUDIOS
Exhibition catalog essay by Donna Gustafon
Printed by the Jane Voorhees Zimmerli Art Museum, Rutgers University
Reproduction: *Gray Stag/Ochre Field,* 1984

1981   THE WORKING PROCESS
Color Reproduction: *Untitled,* 1981

MIXED BAG, image, p12
Exhibition catalog essay by Robert Browning
Printed by the Alternative Museum
Reproduction: *Cumulus on the Mount,* 1981

COVERS

2005   THE NATIONAL ACADEMIES PRESS TRADE OFFERINGS
Published by Joseph Henry Press
Color Reproduction: *Cranes, Warblers and Ironwood,* 2003

2005   THE NATIONAL ACADEMIES PRESS NEW AND FORTHCOMING BOOKS
Published by Joseph Henry Press
Color Reproduction: *Shore Site,* 2005

1996   LEGACY FOUNDATION
Color Reproduction: *Good Medicine,* monoprint, chine colle, 1996

2017   INTERNATIONAL JOURNAL OF VISUAL ARTS: STUDIES AND COMMUNICATION
Volume 20; Number 20, 2017
Published by Dr. Shekhar Chandra Joshi, Almora, Uttarakhand, India
Front Cover Color Reproduction: *Stag in Blue Field,* 2014
Back Cover Color Reproductions: *Kali/Black Madonna,* 1998 and *Valley of Flowers,* 2015

FINE ART PRINT PUBLICATIONS

2013   TANDEM PRESS
Large scale monoprints and lithograph publication

1984-2008   PELAVIN EDITIONS, LTD
Large scale monoprints and etching publication

1983   SOLO PRESS
Mixed media lithograph

BOOK PUBLICATIONS

2017   TWENTY- TWO HORSES, STAGS AND BISON: PAINTINGS
by Valentina DuBasky
Published by Abingdon Square Publishing

2011   NICHOLAS NEVIUS
by Lee Barnes, illustrations by Valentina DuBasky
Published by Abingdon Square Publishing

2009   THE CAMBODIAN JOURNAL: DRAWINGS 1994-1998
by Valentina DuBasky
Published by Abingdon Square Publishing

2002   SOUL SURVIVORS: STORIES OF WOMEN & CHILDREN IN CAMBODIA
by Carol Bhavia Wagner, photographs by Valentina DuBasky
Published by Wild Iris Press

LIST OF PLATES

www.ingramcontent.com/pod-product-compliance
Lightning Source LLC
Chambersburg PA
CBHW050439180526
45159CB00006B/2600